VICTORIAN GLORY
IN SAN FRANCISCO AND THE BAY AREA

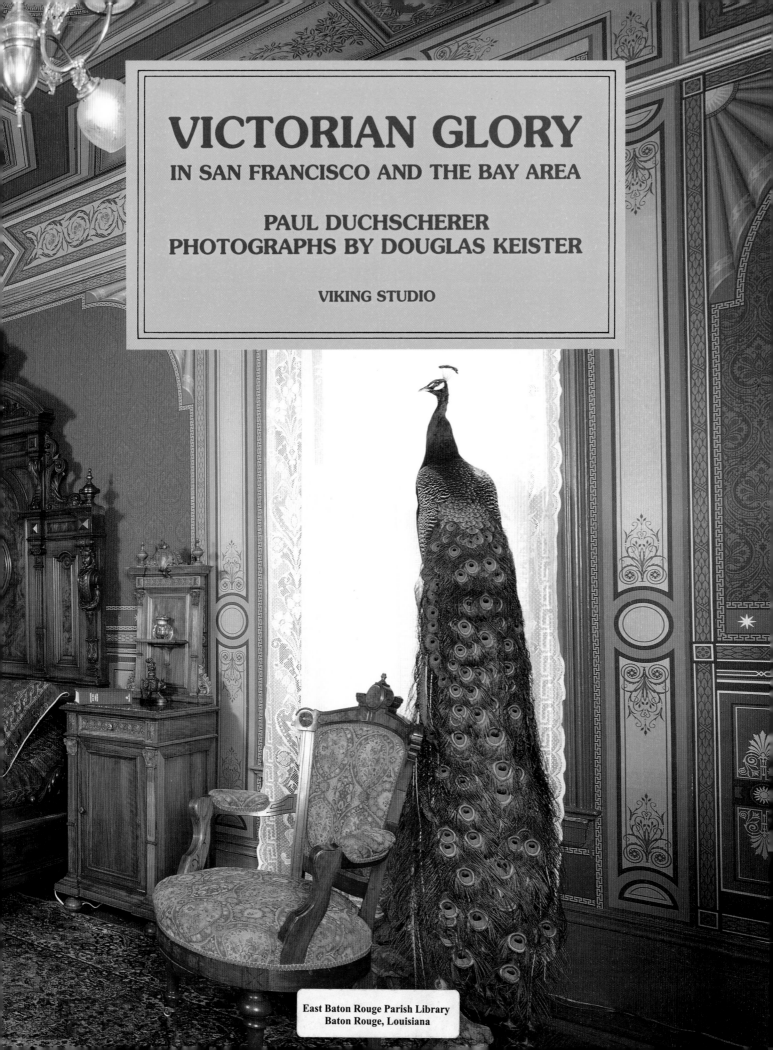

VICTORIAN GLORY
IN SAN FRANCISCO AND THE BAY AREA

PAUL DUCHSCHERER
PHOTOGRAPHS BY DOUGLAS KEISTER

VIKING STUDIO

(*Preceding pages*) Bedroom of an Italianate-style row house, San Francisco (c.1875). Above a double parlor, two second-floor bedrooms of this house were combined to create a master bedroom of grandeur. Reflected in the mirror above the arched-marble fireplace mantel is a slanted bay window facing the street. The corner site provides brilliant light from a pair of south-facing windows, one of which highlights a stuffed peacock with cascading tail feathers, animating the effects of color, pattern, and reflection throughout the room. The scale and architectural quality of the walnut Renaissance Revival furniture provided inspiration for the wallpaper treatment. Based on the room's new proportions, the scheme creates a close relationship between the ceiling and wall elements, helping to fuse the room's complexity into a cohesive whole. Accented with Renaissance Revival-style circular forms and filigree motifs, a wide gold border defines the ceiling panels and window frames. Various wall panels filled with a red damask pattern are topped by a panelized frieze. A dado pattern seen at the far lower right anchors the panels, and fan designs create an arched effect around the room. Giving the appearance of the ceiling being open to the night sky, deep blue panels above the bed are scattered with golden stars.

VIKING STUDIO
Published by the Penguin Group
Penguin Putnam Inc., 375 Hudson Street,
New York, New York 10014, U.S.A.

Penguin Books Ltd, 27 Wrights Lane,
London W8 5TZ, England

Penguin Books Australia Ltd, Ringwood,
Victoria, Australia

Penguin Books Canada Ltd, 10 Alcorn Avenue,
Toronto, Ontario, Canada M4V 3B2

Penguin Books (N.Z.) Ltd, 182-90 Wairau Road,
Auckland 10, New Zealand

Penguin Books Ltd, Registered Offices:
Harmondsworth, Middlesex, England

First published in the United States by Viking Studio,
a member of Penguin Putnam Inc.

First Printing, August 2001

10 9 8 7 6 5 4 3 2 1

CIP data available

Book designed by Marilyn Rey
Printed and bound by Dai Nippon Printing Co., Hong Kong, Ltd.

ISBN: 0-670-89376-5

This book is dedicated to the past, present, and future successes
of historic preservation in the San Francisco Bay Area,
and to fulfilling the ongoing task of public education about the beauty,
value, and significance of historic buildings everywhere.

Acknowledgments

Some of the following names are of those who generously shared their homes with us so that many more could admire and learn from them. Other names are those of others who helped us in many different ways—from sharing location ideas, to providing insight and guidance, to simple inspiration. Each of these contributions is an intrinsic part of what has made this book possible, and to all concerned we offer our heartfelt thanks and appreciation. To others deserving mention who may have been inadvertently omitted, we offer humble apologies with our thanks. Ian Agrell, Alameda Architectural Preservation Society, Alamo Square Neighborhood Association, Beach Alexander, Rob Anderson, Vonne Alvey, Artistic License of San Francisco, Tom Aspeotis / Aspeotis Construction, Dianne Ayres and Timothy Hansen, Bennye and Richard Bail, Gerald Becket and Tom O'Callaghan, Berkeley Architectural Heritage Association / Anthony Bruce, James Bernstein and John Bissell, Vicky and Marshall Berol, Adrienne Bolsega, Helen Boutell, Larry Boyce, Bradbury & Bradbury Art Wallpapers / Bruce Bradbury, Ken Sarna and staff, Gray Brechin, Jane Browne, Peter and Kathleen Bridgman, Bob and Karen Buckter, J. R. Burrows & Company / John Burrows and Dan Cooper, California Historical Society, Camron-Stanford House / Frankie Rhodes and Elizabeth Way, Alice Carey / Carey and Company, Scott Cazet, Barbara and Jack Chambers / The Spencer House, Cohen-Bray House / Victorian Preservation Center of Oakland / Helen, Kenneth, and Chris Gilliland, Barbara and Patty Donald and special thanks to Hank Dunlop for generously sharing his research and knowledge about the Cohen-Bray House, Brian Coleman and Howard Cohen, Phil Diers and Bob Meslinsky, Polly Dinkel and David Baer, Riley Doty, Allen Dragge, Mr. and Mrs. James P. Duchscherer, Kenneth J. Duchscherer, Sandy and Steven P. Duchscherer, Robert Dufort / Magic Brush, Trent Dunphy and Robert Mainardi, Dunsmuir House and Gardens, Inc. / Lynda Guthrie, Teresa Wilkins, Sally Boothby and Dan Petersen, Edelman Productions / Pam Rorke Levy and Cindy Marsh, Lara and Bill Eichenberger, Falkirk Cultural Center / Carol Adney and Jane Lange, Justin Ferate, Cathy Ferron and Paul Roberts, Judy Freed and Barry Hemphill, Bryan Freedman and Ron Gregoire, Friends of the Urban Forest, Ora Gosey, William Grasse, Sibyl Groff, George Gunn, Sharon and Jim Hendley, Denise, Keith, and Stephanie Hice, High Noon Productions / Orin Levy and Laura Gillespie, Judith Hoyem, The Inn San Francisco / Connie Wu and Marty Neely, Skeeter Jones / Clearheart, Katherine Keister, Virginia and David Keller, David Kessler, Leslie and John Koelsch, Lorna Kollmeyer, Erik Kramvik and Roger Fong, Craig Kuhns, Norman Larson, Lathrop House / Redwood City Heritage Association, Jeanne and Mark Lazzarini, Judith Lynch and Richard Knight, Marin County Historical Society / Boyd Gate House Museum / Gerald J. Kobil, McConaghy House / Esther Jorgensen and Marlene Willard, McMullen House / Kathy, Leroy, and Camlo Looper, Carol Mead / Carol Mead Design, Pauline Metcalf, Meyers House and Garden Museum, David Modell, Fumi Momota, Mosswood Park / Perri Walker and Cassie Lopez, Brian Murrian, John Muir National Historic Site / David K. Blackburn, Bruce Nelson / Local Color, Ruby Newman, The Nob Hill Inn, Karen and Ralph Noistering, Oakland Heritage Alliance / Jo Ann Coleman, Octagon House and The National Society of Colonial Dames of America in California / Nancy Weston, Old House Interiors / Gloucester Publishers / Patricia Poore, William O'Donnell and staff, Old House Journal / Hanley Wood, Inc. / Gordon Bock and staff, Pardee Home Museum / David A. Nicolai, George W. Patterson House / Ardenwood East Bay Regional Park / Fran Bartocek, Joseph Pecora, Peralta Adobe and Fallon House Historic Site / San Jose Historical Museums / Cecilia Clark, Margaret and Scott Peterson, Jill Pilaroscia, Jane Powell / House Dressing, Dana Ralls and Philip Vick, Red Victorian Bed & Breakfast Inn / Sami Sunchild, Gail Redman, Rengstorff House / Ginny Kaminski, Richardson Bay Audubon Center and Sanctuary / Lyford House / Marty Fujita, Richard Reutlinger / Brune-Reutlinger House, Debra Richards, Melodie and Chris Rufer, Stephen Rynerson and Pat O'Brien / Rynerson-O'Brien Architects, Julie, Robert, and Lupe Sanchez, San Francisco Architectural Heritage / Haas-Lilienthal House / Lyla Max and John Gaul, San Francisco Beautiful, San Francisco Historical Society, Scripps Productions / Karen Meissner, Jim Seigel, Michael Shannon / Shannon-Kavanaugh House, Sherman House Hotel, James Shinn House, Maggie and Stuart Stark / Charles Rupert Designs, Lawrence Sullivan, Pat Suzuki, The Swedenborgian Church / Reverend James Lawrence, Keith Tartler, This Old House / Bruce Irving and Russ Morash, Therese Tierney, Traditional Building and Period Homes / Clem Labine and Judith Leif, General Mariano Vallejo Home State Historic Park / Roy Flatt, Michelle Kazeminejad and Scott Pace, Vedanta Society of Northern California, Paul Vestal and Hollis Hardin, Victorian Alliance, Victorian Preservation Association of San Jose / Matt and Lori Knowles, The Victorian Society in America and the San Francisco Chapter, Captain Walsh House Bed & Breakfast Inn / Reed and Steven Robbins, Connie and Rob Weaver, Webster House Bed & Breakfast Inn / Susan and Andrew McCormack, Keith Williams, and Bathsheba Malsheen, Richard Guy Wilson, Winans Construction / Nina and Paul Winans, Winchester Mystery House / Shozo Kagoshima and Warren Weitzel, Jan Winford, Diana Woodbridge, Scott Wynn, Ron Yamamoto, Kenneth Yee, Gary Yuschalk and Larkin Mayo / Victorian Interiors, Laura and Bert Zaccaria, George Zaffle, Richard and Cher Zillman, Debey Zito and Terry Schmitt.

We wish to extend particular thanks and appreciation to our talented, tireless, and compassionate editor, Cyril Nelson, whose discerning guidance speaks for itself. Also due special thanks is our literary agent, Julie Castiglia / The Castiglia Agency, who contributed prudent professional advice. Finally, for every step of the way, there was Sandy Schweitzer, John Freed, and Don Merrill to help us in endless ways, and to each of them goes our endless gratitude for all their patience, kindness, and support.

Contents

Preface

Musings on San Francisco, the Bay Area, Victorian Homes, and This Book

A UNIVERSAL MAGNET

Whether or not they have actually visited here, many Americans regard San Francisco and the entire Bay Area as familiar territory. Awareness of the region and the sense of place it evokes seem to be commonplace not only across the country, but also around the world. What is even more remarkable is that San Francisco was almost as widely known during much of the Victorian period as it is today.

One frequently cited reason for its being a cynosure is the area's popularity as a location for movies, television, and commercial advertising. Promotion of tourism in San Francisco and the Bay Area is another reason for its popularity. While tourism has been San Francisco's top money-maker for many years, it is also a growing business for such nearby locales as the wine country of Napa and Sonoma counties, the rugged coastline, and the giant trees of the so-called Redwood Empire.

From its beginnings as an outpost of civility in the wilderness, San Francisco quickly established high standards of hospitality and fine food that have earned it the long-held distinction of having more restaurants per capita than any other American city. The spirit of its bawdy past is kept alive by its innumerable bars, thus sealing its reputation as a "serious" party town.

Never a place to sell itself short, San Francisco was for many years marketed to the world as "the city that knows how," until that was eventually eclipsed by the more inclusive phrase "everybody's favorite city." With mostly romantic references to the City by the Bay, a wide range of popular music has been created over the years. Of these, only the City's official song, "I Left My Heart in San Francisco" (released and sung in the early 1960s by Tony Bennett) has achieved the status of a "classic standard" today. Some would certainly argue that the runner-up, "San Francisco," made famous by Jeanette MacDonald in the 1936 movie of the same name, fully deserves the top spot.

A PORT IN THE STORM

Ever since the boom years of the Gold Rush, the character of San Francisco has been defined by an exceptional cultural diversity. As the traditional West Coast counterpart to

New York City, it too can be described as a "melting pot" of many immigrant cultures. Because of the rapid urban development that occurred so early in its history, the City provided plentiful economic opportunities for those willing and able to locate here.

The common outside impression of the San Francisco Bay Area as a haven of personal freedom and self-expression has helped galvanize its reputation as a bastion of socially progressive thinking, which might be debatable. However, despite another common impression that much of the local population must be either social misfits or mad eccentrics, the Bay Area has consistently attracted many luminaries of the art and literary worlds to settle here. Thus there was the early development of a strong, long-standing tradition of public encouragement and support of the arts.

For many, the area's pervasive "live-and-let-live" atmosphere created a safe place for people to live out their dreams. Long before the literary waves of the late 1950s "Beat" generation emerged out of San Francisco's North Beach, or the early 1960s emergence of Berkeley's student activisim and its "Free Speech" movement, or the more freewheeling cultural implications of the "Hippie" generation in the later 1960s, there has been a well-established public tolerance for what might elsewhere be considered too extreme or unconventional to be "acceptable" social behavior.

Perhaps there is something about the allure of life on the western edge of the continent that fosters an intangible sense of exhilaration and even optimism. As a motivating force, this sense of "now or never" may have heightened the expectations and sharpened the hopes of many who followed their dreams here. Although success stories abound, not all who came were destined to find the pot of gold or promised land they were seeking. So an old lesson emerges: it is people, not places, that make (or break) dreams.

THE BAY AREA'S VICTORIAN LEGACY

Few cities can claim the instantaneous association with Victoriana enjoyed by the city of San Francisco. This is not simply due to the large number of Victorian houses that remain here; it is rather their cumulative visual impact, when viewed in a densely urban context, that is so compelling. Resolutely proclaiming "San Francisco," these houses impart a jaunty rhythm and an inviting human scale to the hilly streetscapes of the City.

San Francisco, for all its celebrated charms, cannot lay claim to every significant Victorian house in the Bay Area, for many of the finest surviving examples can be found down the Peninsula to the south, as well as across the Bay to the north and east. Although comparatively few local residents (and even fewer visitors) are particularly aware of them, these homes are as reflective of their community's evolution and as steeped in colorful family histories, as any of their more famous City counterparts.

Overshadowed by the dazzle of San Francisco, many less-celebrated Bay Area communities are long overdue for greater public recognition of their own remarkable examples of nineteenth-century domestic architecture. Quite unlike the wall-to-wall row house development that typifies the tighter confines of San Francisco, most of these nearby Victorian houses were built on much larger plots of land. While the settings of many have since been compromised by urban sprawl, some were actually built as farmhouses or rural country retreats for the well-to-do.

Because of its quintessentially Victorian reputation, many visitors to San Francisco are eager to visit these homes, only to be surprised to learn that San Francisco has only two house museums that are open to the public. However, there are quite a number of Victorian house museums that are waiting to be discovered and enjoyed in nearby Bay Area communities. To help readers locate these house museums, a list (including a few not pictured) has been provided at the back of this book.

A number of these Bay Area houses have not been extensively photographed or previously published in color; thus it has been a goal of this book to document them inside and out as thoroughly as possible. It is hoped that the resulting increased visibility and public awareness will lead to greater attendance and financial support, as well as the opportunity for study, enjoyment, and inspiration that only such a firsthand experience can bring.

ABOUT THIS BOOK

The Introduction begins with a historic overview of the development of the area, with a particular emphasis on San Francisco from the period of its Native American population to its settlement as a missionary outpost. It continues through the years when it was known as the village of Yerba Buena, through its official emergence as the city of San Francisco, to its transformation almost overnight by the Gold Rush into a major port of call. Leading up to the turn of the century, the ensuing decades of the City's

growth comprise the period during which most of the houses in this book were built. The Victorian city of San Francisco was soon to be transformed again by the great earthquake and fire of 1906, and also by the changing times that the new century set into motion. This overview is illustrated with a number of archival drawings and photographs including some from the 1906 disaster. Concluding the Introduction are some reflections on preservation, as well as discovering and looking at old houses.

Following this is a chapter called "Victorian House Planning" that discusses the ways that typical housing forms in Victorian San Francisco were conceived and planned, as well as how they were used by their residents. Comparisons are made between a selection of three representative city dwellings: for working-class and for middle- and upper-class citizens. Each example is illustrated by drawings of the period, showing floor plans and exterior elevations.

The basis for most of this book's photographs is a series of chapters that trace the procession of shifting architectural styles that took root in the Bay Area during the course of the nineteenth century: Gothic Revival, Italianate, Second Empire, Stick/Eastlake, Queen Anne, Colonial Revival, and Shingle styles. Pertinent archival drawings as well as examples of representative interiors are included in each chapter along with a wider range of exterior photos. It should be noted that some of the interiors shown in these chapters are considered high-style examples that were created for wealthy households. The typical San Francisco row houses that were often built by developers as speculative housing for the working- and middle-class homeowner usually had rather standardized interior detailing.

It sometimes happens that Victorian houses are not easy to categorize, so the Hybrid Styles chapter shows homes the architecture of which simply defies stylistic logic and may combine the characteristics of at least two (or perhaps several) styles.

As a postscript to the Victorian era, the chapter on Edwardian-era style illustrates home and apartment design that typified new construction in early twentieth-century San Francisco, such as the housing that was put up quickly during the years immediately following the great earthquake and fire of 1906.

The success stories found in the Before and After chapter will hopefully inspire homeowners and design professionals alike. These examples demonstrate that a new lease on life is always possible for even the worst-looking house on the block. The impressive skills of contemporary craftspeople that we illustrate here prove that they can still "build 'em like they used to."

In Victorian Revival Interiors we show rooms that exemplify the interpretive approach to historic design that characterizes much of the current Victorian Revival movement. Rather than attempt to recreate something that is historically exact, these rooms have the vitality and animation that one can achieve through a creative approach that is probably best described as adaptation. While such rooms remain true to the spirit of their nineteenth-century models, something fresh is created in the process as the rooms harmoniously develop into a kind of environmental tapestry, where the "whole is greater than the sum of its parts."

Each chapter of this book is intended to encourage the reader's further exploration of Victorian styles as the essential characteristics become more familiar. If this book is successful in providing a basic visual knowledge of complex local house styles to the uninitiated, merely curious, or somewhat rusty Victorian house afficionado, then it will have fulfilled one of its primary intentions. Much of the background that readers may gain here about Victorian house styles will also enhance old-house sightseeing elsewhere in America.

The photographs in this book document an important range of period structures along with a number of their intact interiors, and we hope it will advance the pursuit of further studies by others on the subject. For architects, interior designers, and contractors who may be involved in restoring or renovating Victorian houses now or in the future this book can function as a working tool. Because its images depict many parts and details of historic architecture, these can potentially be recycled as part of an active design repertoire.

Another significant goal of the book is to emphasize the importance of historic preservation in twenty-first-century America. To nurture it today is to encourage it to flourish in the years ahead. While we have become more skillful at making some of our new buildings look old, we must also understand that the richness and diversity of our surviving architectural heritage is a finite and irreplaceable resource. The loss of these buildings due to poor planning, misguided judgment, or misunderstood priorities must not take place.

Historic preservation must be given national importance in the twenty-first century.

A PERSONAL NOTE

My fascination with old buildings, both inside and out, has been continuous throughout my life thanks to the unhesitating encouragement of my parents and my two brothers who shared my love of old buildings, and the stories, furnishings, and other memorabilia that accompanied them. Despite our family's relocation around the country six times during my childhood due to my father's job transfers, I had the benefit of growing up in a household that treasured the traditions of the past. A high priority was given to the importance of preserving family customs, particularly at holidays, as well as instilling respect for cherished family heirlooms. In our household, what we called antique was invariably Victorian.

Most of my adult life has been spent in San Francisco—this magical and eminently liveable place—and my enthusiasm remains undiminished.

Like so many others who come here, the Victorian houses were an intrinsic part of my earliest impressions of the City, and I was immediately beguiled by them. Many years later, while teaching classes about the history of architecture and interiors, I enjoyed being able to include Victorian homes in my slide lectures. Through my work as an interior designer, I have been privileged to visit many fine local examples, some of which are included here.

I should note that *Victorian Glory* succeeds three books on American bungalows co-authored with photographer Douglas Keister, in which we discuss and illustrate the architecture, interiors, and gardens of these little houses of the early twentieth-century Arts and Crafts style. They are the houses that were once considered a modern antidote to Victorian homes, and which were considered outdated and impractical by many turn-of-the-century Americans. Today, far less celebrated (or preserved) as historic houses than Victorians, bungalows have become important to preservationists.

Regardless of their period or style, old houses that are honored in their communities can become their own best advertising for the cause of historic preservation. More of us must learn that these survivors are important assets to our streetscapes and not liabilities to be eliminated or replaced. For my part, covering a subject close to my heart has proven both a creative opportunity and luxury I have savored. When I began *Victorian Glory*, I felt quite familiar with the subject of Victorian houses. It was the unexpected surprises along the way that reminded me of how new discoveries are often waiting in our own backyard if we only take the time to look for and recognize them.

PAUL DUCHSCHERER

Introduction

New Spain to the Gold Rush
Overview of Local History and Lore

THE MYTH OF CALIFORNIA

As befits a place associated with romance and mystery, California's name is derived from that of a legendary island described in the writings of the Spanish novelist Garcí Rodríguez Ordóñez de Montalvo. In his novel of around 1510, *Las Sergas de Espandían,* it states "that on the right hand of the Indies there is an island called California, very near the Terrestrial Paradise . . ." This island was supposedly rich in gold, populated by a race of Amazons, and described as having "bold rocks and crags" plus mythic winged creatures called griffins. By the 1540s, the name was in common use for a real location in New Spain—Baja ("lower") California. That region's physical resemblance to the island described in the novel was the likely reason for the association. However, California's gold was long to remain merely wishful thinking.

EARLY EXPLORERS AND DISCOVERY OF SAN FRANCISCO BAY

It seems strange that the presence of such an enormous sheltered harbor as San Francisco Bay could have remained unknown to foreign explorers for as long as it did. There were several times over a period of almost three centuries that it came very close to being discovered, but remained hidden—quite possibly behind a mantle of fog. Even if the weather had been clear, sight of it may also have been obscured due to the narrowness of the strait leading into the Bay, which was later dubbed the Golden Gate. For a vessel at sea, only a ship's momentary alignment with the strait would allow a clear view of the opening. The Bay's entrance may also have been further obscured by the screening effect of its islands and the backdrop of hills to the east. Once a ship moved past it, the Golden Gate would be quickly blocked from view by the steep bluffs that line its length, and soon make it appear as little more than a dent in the coastline. The Bay's sequestered location ensured the local Native Americans an extended period of peace and privacy from the outside world.

The first European explorers of the region were the Spanish, who, under the leadership of Hernán Cortes, landed on the east coast of Mexico in 1519 and soon established their colony of New Spain. They were motivated by a search for gold and other riches, which they believed was theirs for the taking in the New World. Driven more by hearsay and legend than reality, their dreams were fulfilled within two years after their arrival with a looting spree that began with the conquest of the treasure-laden Aztec city of Tenochtitlán in Mexico. About the same time Francisco Pizarro conquered Peru's Inca empire, which yielded even more spectacular golden treasures. Word of this bounty spread rapidly throughout Europe.

The first time a European navigator is known to have passed by the Golden Gate was in 1542. Sailing on the *San*

1. *(Opposite)* San Francisco row houses (c.1885). In a typical cityscape of contrasts between old and new, this trio stands out sharply against its more modern neighbors. Like many of the City's Victorian homes, their style could be described as hybrid, for each has elements of more than one style. At the right, two twin houses have a bit of the Italianate style in their angled bay windows, pediments, and window hoods, yet the vertical detailing around the windows and squared upper cornice suggest the Stick style. More typical of the Queen Anne style is how the squared roofline is supported by brackets and hangs out over the slanted bays. The house on the left, which was recently restored, combines Italianate style with Queen Anne and Stick/Eastlake-style details. The result of a Spanish-style makeover in the 1930s, this house was completely encased in stucco. Careful removal of the stucco revealed outlines in the old paint where a wealth of wooden details had been removed. Thus it was the house that helped guide its accurate restoration.

2. View of "Postcard Row" on Alamo Square, San Francisco (1894–1895). Developed by Matthew Cavanaugh as speculative housing, this famous row of Queen Anne houses includes at the far left the turreted example that Cavanaugh built for himself. This row enjoys two views: in front, Alamo Square; and behind, the downtown skyline. Alamo Square is one of three public parks dedicated in 1858 within the Western Addition area, which was officially annexed to the City in 1865.

3. Conservatory in Golden Gate Park, San Francisco (c.1879). This exceptional building, made of California redwood and glass, was originally commissioned by James Lick, a Bay Area millionaire-philanthropist, who supposedly intended to erect it on his property in San Jose. However, at the time of his death in 1876, the wooden crates containing the prefabricated building were still unopened. A group of wealthy San Franciscans bought the building, and it was finally erected in 1879 in newly developed Golden Gate Park. Severe storm damage in the mid-1990s caused its prolonged closure to the public; a comprehensive restoration is underway.

Salvador under the Spanish flag, a Portuguese explorer named Juan Rodríguez Cabrillo was searching for possible water routes across North America, and his voyage was also the first to carry the name of California so far north. Based on cartographer's records, his ship must have passed close by the Golden Gate twice in the fall of that year: first while traveling north as far as today's Point Arena, and again on the return trip to the south. Such voyages were hazardous, and Cabrillo was to die from an arm injury incurred during the return trip. In January 1543, he was buried on San Miguel, one of the Channel Islands off the southern coast of California.

That spring, his pilot Bartolomé Ferrelo resumed Cabrillo's investigative surveying expedition for Spain, returning farther up the California coast and sailing as far as today's California–Oregon border. Like his late commander, Ferrelo was also to pass twice by the entrance to San Francisco Bay without realizing it. We know from his cartographer's charting of the Farallon Islands, which lie nearly thirty miles out to sea opposite the Golden Gate, that he came quite close.

Another thirty-seven years would pass before San Francisco Bay was to have its next close brush with discovery. In June 1579, the Englishman Francis Drake (later knighted as Sir Francis Drake by Queen Elizabeth I) reached northern California waters. His ship the *Golden Hind* was loaded down with an impressive booty he had looted from different Spanish ports and galleons off the west coast of South America. At a spot generally believed to be a curving inlet north of the Golden Gate in today's Marin County (later named Drake's Bay), he decided to beach his ship for repairs, rest his crew, and make preparations for the long voyage home to England.

Drake's party remained ashore for about six weeks, during which they apparently received a friendly reception by the Coast Miwok tribe. If they indeed landed at today's Drake's Bay, they probably didn't venture much closer to San Francisco Bay from their landing place. Coastal mountains and distance would seem to have made that unlikely. We know that before he left California, Drake laid claim to the entire region in the name of Queen Elizabeth and England. Calling it Nova Albion, he engraved the name on a brass plate that he attached to a wooden post. Although not forgotten, his claim was never to be actively pursued by the English.

In the mid-1930s, only a few miles from the presumed location of Drake's landing, a weathered brass plate was discovered in Marin County. Crudely but legibly engraved and signed with Drake's name, it stated his claim of New Albion for England, and was dated June 17, 1579. Now housed in Berkeley's Bancroft Library, the authenticity of this fascinating artifact has been the subject of ongoing debate. However, Drake's landing somewhere in the vicinity and his land claim remain documented facts.

It is probable that the shores of present-day Drake's Bay were the landfall for the *Golden Hind*, especially in light of notes made by the ship's Chaplain Fletcher about the "white bancks and cliffs" where they landed that reminded him of England's chalky-white cliffs of Dover. Drake's Bay is indeed bordered by light-colored cliffs that are quite specific to this particular location.

Succeeding Drake, the next navigator known to have passed by San Francisco Bay was Sebastián Rodríguez Cermeño, a Portuguese who was sailing for Spain. In November 1595, in advance of other Spanish galleons returning from Asia with goods headed for Mexico, he was in the area with his ship the *San Augustín,* which was overloaded with precious cargo from the Philippines. Like Drake, he was in search of a safe harbor suitable for making repairs to his ship and resting its crew. In fact, he is believed to have found the very same beach where Drake had presumably landed over fifteen years earlier. Fate was less kind to Cermeño's party, for within a few weeks after landing a severe storm that lashed the coast also managed to dislodge and destroy his ship and its valuable cargo, and even kill some crew members. His spirit broken, he was able to retreat with the survivors to Mexico on a small salvaged launch.

Seven years passed before another attempt was made to find a safe harbor in the region for the Spanish trading galleons. In 1602, Sebastián Vizcaíno sailed up the California coast, but still failed to find San Francisco Bay. However, he managed carefully to chart and name many features of the coastline, including Point Reyes close to Drake's Bay. Eventually landing on the shores of what is now Monterey Bay, Vizcaíno was the first to claim this area for the Spanish king. A long-circulated account of his expedition, and particularly of Monterey Bay, spoke of the region's many attributes and of its future promise. Yet, with the departure of his ship, over one hundred fifty years were to pass before Spain's further exploration of Alta ("upper") California would resume. The reasons for this extended absence were chiefly due to a shift in Spain's interest from California to focus on the conquest and colonization of Central and South America.

Finally, their interest was revived by fears of Russian advancement into California from the north, where they had already established trading centers on the Alaskan peninsula. There was also the possibility of England pressing its claim to the New Albion staked by Francis Drake in 1579. Even France was considered a possible competitor for the region. Reactions to these threats finally brought California out of obscurity, and the wheel of change for the Bay Area was again set in motion. No one could have predicted that within a hundred years the California Gold Rush would not only put San Francisco on the map but would also create the most vibrant city on America's western frontier.

The peninsula known as Baja California was long thought to be the southern end of a larger island, and Spanish explorations to the north that would prove otherwise were plagued by the inhospitable barren desert that was encountered. It was not until 1701 that Baja California was officially confirmed as a long peninsula attached to the northern mainland.

Spain's renewed concern about the region to the north was not only political, but the potential bounties of California's mineral resources were also a motive, and something needed to be done. On the order of Spanish King Carlos III, plans were made to colonize Alta California: the first step was to send north four exploratory parties of soldiers, priests, and civilians, with two assigned to the land, and two to sea routes.

These expeditions set out in 1769 under the leadership of Don Gaspar de Portolá, a captain in the Spanish army, who was also named as governor of both Alta and Baja California. With considerable effort, the divergent groups finally all met at San Diego Bay, to recover, regroup, and resume their efforts. Despite the trials of their journey, Portolá was anxious to push onward, intent on finding the same Monterey Bay admired by Vizcaíno one hundred fifty years earlier, where he hoped to establish his provincial capital.

It was in San Diego, at that same time, that Father Junípero Serra of the Franciscan order blessed the future site of the Mission San Diego de Alcalá, which was to establish the first link in a chain of twenty-one missions that were soon to be established along the coast of California. They brought useful agricultural practices into California at an early date, accelerating its remarkable potential for what was to become a pivotal industry. The actual construction of the San Diego mission commenced as Portolá pressed on in search of Monterey.

The cultural significance of the mission system on the Native American tribes was devastating, for the central purpose of the missions was to convert these "infidels" to Christianity. Part of the program was also to educate and train them in European culture and dress. Native Americans would provide much of the workforce necessary for farming and tending livestock that would support each mission community. Subsequently, many became overly dependent on the Franciscans for their direction and livelihood, and were unable to regain their lost sense of tribal identity when the security of the mission system eventually faltered.

The first party of Europeans to travel by land up the California coast, Portolá and his men were necessarily forced to turn inland when confronted with mountains that plunged into the Pacific. For this reason, they were unable to locate some coastal landmarks, noted long ago by Vizcaíno, that would have led them directly to Monterey. By skirting the mountains that ring it on the east, they unknowingly passed it by and continued their search northward. Once back along the coastline, they reached the lower part of the San Francisco peninsula, where again steep cliffs dropping into the ocean blocked their forward progress. At this point they still believed that Monterey lay ahead; Portolá sent several men up what is now called Mount Montara to get a sense of what lay ahead.

As a result, they sighted the Farallon Islands and Point Reyes (both recognizable from Vizcaíno's maps), which told them they had overshot Monterey by a considerable distance;

San Francisco Bay was still blocked from view by mountains to the east. Disappointed and frustrated, Portolá decided that as long as they had come this far his group would proceed to Point Reyes, which their maps told them was not very far ahead. Portolá sent his chief scout, Sergeant José Ortega, and a small exploratory group to go ahead and plan the best route.

Proceeding north and trekking up the long sandy stretch of what is today's Ocean Beach, Ortega and his men managed to reach the very top of the San Francisco peninsula. Shortly after passing the landmark now called Seal Rocks, they realized that a narrow arm of the sea was completely blocking their progress further north to Point Reyes. It was the Golden Gate. Proceeding further to a ridgetop, probably near what is now the location of the Golden Gate Bridge, they were able to see what had been hidden for centuries—San Francisco Bay. As they gazed over its shining reaches, the vast scale of its island-dotted expanse made it seem more like an inland sea than any harbor they knew.

It seems curiously anticlimactic that apparently they considered the great Bay to be just a disappointing barrier to their northerly progress, rather than a momentous discovery. Ortega's party returned to Portolá's camp only to find that a hunting party had made the same discovery.

Trekking higher up Mount Montara in search of provisions, Portolá's hunting party was able to see over the hills that had previously blocked their view to the east, and they saw the southern reaches of San Francisco Bay that extend toward the Santa Clara Valley. Returning to the south, they were at last able to locate Monterey Bay, on whose shores was destined to rise the colonial capital of Alta California.

When Portolá returned to Monterey in the spring of 1770, accompanied by Father Junípero Serra and another Franciscan priest, Juan Crespi, he decided to build there both a presidio (military post) and another mission. To solemnize that plan a ceremony was conducted under the same ancient oak where Sebastián Vizcaíno supposedly stood as he claimed possession of the region for Spain so many years earlier.

Once again it was time to move north and explore more fully San Francisco Bay and its surrounding countryside, this time with an eye toward the possibility of Spanish colonization there. However, in an age and place when everything was subject to seemingly interminable delays, it would be almost another six years before a permanent settlement was established at San Francisco.

THE SAN FRANCISCO BAY AREA'S EARLIEST RESIDENTS

The Spanish colonials found a series of well-established, peaceful, and friendly communities of Native Americans waiting for them with a simple but intact culture that went back thousands of years. The earliest Spanish explorers dubbed them Los Costenos, or the Coastal People. They were also called Costanoans, and the tribal name Ohlones has recently been suggested as being more appropriate.

4. Gazebo at Sutro Heights, San Francisco (c.1885). This is the solitary remnant of the manicured gardens of a now-vanished estate belonging to Adolph Sutro (1830–1898), a Prussian immigrant trained in mining engineering who arrived during the Gold Rush, and later became rich from important innovations he developed for Nevada's silver-mining industry. A major landowner in San Francisco, he was also a scholar who purportedly had an extraordinary private library that was destroyed in the 1906 fire.

5. Mission Dolores in 1856, San Francisco (1791). Construction of Mission Dolores began in 1782, when California was still a remote outpost of New Spain. Under the direction of the Franciscan padres, the mission's mud-and-straw adobe bricks were made by local Native Americans. This photograph shows the Mission's dilapidated condition in the mid-nineteenth century, when its once-thriving agricultural community was largely diminished. In 1918, Mission Dolores was sensitively restored under the direction of noted Bay Area architect Willis Polk.

6. View of San Francisco's waterfront in 1850. During a visit to the Gold Rush boomtown, Francis S. Marryat sketched this revealing scene near the present-day corner of Clay and Sansome Streets. Today, this location is several blocks inland from the Bay. The drawing later appeared in Marryat's 1855 book *Mountains and Molehills*. The massive influx of ships that jammed the City's harbor during the Gold Rush caused the shoreline to be extended at a dizzying rate by both landfill and wharf construction. Many vessels were literally abandoned in place by impatient arrivals eager to reach the gold fields. Named after the ship visible beneath it, the flag-flying Niantic Hotel (and a similar structure at the left) shows the adaptive reuse of such ships that were permanently anchored with landfill. Recently, identifiable remains of the *Niantic* were unearthed during construction of a highrise office tower on the site.

9

Separated from the San Francisco peninsula by the deep channel of the Golden Gate, another local tribe, the Coast Miwok, lived mostly in and around the reaches of present-day Marin County. Other Bay Area tribes included the Wintuns, who lived along the north shore of San Pablo Bay, and the Yokuts, who were located in the areas along the East Bay south of the Carquinez Strait.

SPANISH SETTLEMENT OF SAN FRANCISCO

In 1774, a recently appointed viceroy of New Spain named Antonio Bucareli ordered an outpost to be established on San Francisco Bay, and Captain Don Juan Bautista de Anza was put in charge of leading the process of colonization of the settlement that would become San Francisco. In the spring of 1775, he began assembling from the province of Sonora in northern Mexico a large group of civilians that was willing to relocate together with sufficient supplies, tools, and livestock to sustain their journey and to help establish their new home. Some would remain in Monterey, while others would continue north to the Bay Area. In the fall of 1775, a company of about two hundred forty men, women, and children, along with their leader and enough soldiers to ensure their protection, left Mexico. While the party regrouped along the way, de Anza went ahead to inspect the landscape and select appropriate locations for the Presidio and mission, which they marked with simple white crosses.

In the meantime, a supply ship named *San Carlos* was orderd by Bucareli to explore further and chart San Francisco Bay. Guided by Captain Manuel de Alaya and his chief pilot and cartographer José de Canizares, the ship sailed through the Golden Gate in advance of the colonists' arrival in early August 1775. The next six weeks were spent touring the waters, mapping the region in great detail, and assigning names to prominent features.

On June 29, 1776, Father Francisco Palou conducted mass on the shores of a small lagoon (now disappeared) and gave the new mission its name: San Francisco de Asís in honor of the Franciscan Order's patron saint. As it later became known, Mission Dolores was the sixth mission to be founded in the Franciscan chain. The first building remained in service only until 1782, when the adobe-walled structure that remains standing today was begun. Along with the much-remodeled commandant's house in San Francisco's Presidio, it remains one of the City's architectural links to its earliest years of Spanish occupation.

Despite the implications to their fragile culture, the native Costanoans, who first inhabited the San Francisco peninsula, willingly accepted the mission padres's offers of shelter, clothing, and food in exchange for participation in various tasks, such as making adobe bricks for buildings, working in the mission's vegetable gardens, and tending its livestock. They also learned to weave woolen cloth and attended the mission's religious ceremonies. Although the padres were strict taskmasters, they allowed their wards a two-week annual leave. While most came back to the mission after the two weeks often bringing new recruits with them, others reverted to their former lives, habits, and hunting grounds and chose never to return. Nevertheless Mission Dolores long remained the most important settlement north of Monterey.

Trade restrictions stymied growth in the Bay Area as long as they were in force. When Mexico finally gained its independence from Spain in 1821, it retained California as part of its territory and continued the Spanish policy of prohibiting foreigners and their vessels from visiting and trading in San Francisco. Overall, however, the effect of Mexican independence was one of increasing neglect of the settlement. Visitors to the area made note of the Presidio's dilapidated buildings as early as 1825.

First taking effect in 1834, Governor José Figueroa's Secularizaton Act effectively ended the Franciscan missions. The friars were replaced by secular priests, and all of the California missions were converted to parish churches. The natives were released from being wards of the Franciscans, and the mission properties were divided up and doled out in parcels of land and livestock for each family. While conceived as a well-meaning act of reform, it not only destroyed the Franciscans' mission system, but turned out to be bad news for most of the natives, who, typically, were cheated out of the land they had been promised.

A new development in the Bay Area that was to help improve the local economy was the rise of a great number of cattle ranchos, which during Spanish rule had been severely restricted. The result of the Mexican government having issued a rash of new grazing permits (or land grants), these ranchos, comprising some eight million acres of pasture land, were responsible for a surge in surplus cattle. The by-products of hide and tallow were to prove a significant boon to the local trading market. Seemingly at one of its weakest moments, times of prosperity at last began to emerge in San Francisco.

THE PIONEERS OF YERBA BUENA VILLAGE

The first steps toward a city government began in 1834, when the first ayuntamiento (town council) was organized, and the first alcalde (equivalent of mayor), Francisco de Haro, was appointed. At this time, the small settlement of San Francisco was called Yerba Buena, or "good herb," after a fragrant native plant of the mint family. However, orders still came from the Mexican government in Monterey. One of the first projects was to develop a port on a parcel of government-claimed land that extended some six hundred yards inland from the waterfront.

The balance of the land was to be surveyed as a town site. De Haro had some help from a local resident named William Richardson, an Englishman who had arrived in the area on a British whaling ship in 1822. He would prove to be a pivotal

7. View of San Francisco in 1852. This panorama, looking east from what was later called Nob Hill, shows the widespread development triggered by the onset of the Gold Rush. The harbor is crammed with anchored ships in front of Yerba Buena Island (today the middle anchorage of the Bay Bridge). The backdrop of the East Bay hills will soon contain Oakland and Berkeley. The frontier village of Yerba Buena officially changed its name to San Francisco in 1847. Down the hill at the left the large public building with a cupola and flag is the Jenny Lind Theatre. Sited on Portsmouth Square, the early settlement's epicenter, the theatre was converted to City Hall in 1852 and remained so for twenty years.

8. San Francisco's first cable car (1873). Photographed on the day of its first trial trip, the cable car would transform the City's previously inaccessible hills into locations for the most desirable residential real estate. Its inventor, a Scottish engineer named Andrew S. Hallidie (seated front and center with his wife) was long involved with the mining business; he had devised an innovative aerial-tramway system to transport quantities of ore, lumber, and other supplies over mountain canyons. In 1857, as a replacement for the hemp rope used for hoisting in mines, Hallidie invented a flat rope made of woven wire. Along with fellow engineer Benjamin Brooks, and inspired by the same technology developed for the mining industry, he conceived of an "endless wire ropeway" to be suppressed in a slot below the street so as to propel passenger cars up and down steep hills. The Clay Street Hill Railroad Company was one of eight privately owned cable-car lines in San Francisco, which at their peak covered a total of 112 miles of slotted track. Ascending 307 vertical feet, this line started at Clay and Kearny at Portsmouth Square, passed through Chinatown, up and over the top of Nob Hill, to its terminus at Leavenworth Street on the far western slope.

9. Nob Hill mansions in San Francisco (c.1870s). Once the cable car allowed easy access to its great height and views, the central location of Nob Hill quickly became the most fashionable address in town. Facing California Street, these two mansions were built at its intersection with Taylor Street, and were the epitome of conspicuous consumption. Most such homes were constructed of wood, but then generally painted to resemble stone. The massive Italianate "box" at the right built by the prominent railroad attorney General David D. Colton is a prime example of stone-painted wood. Like most Nob Hill mansions, it was destroyed in the 1906 earthquake and fire; today, its site is occupied by a delightful urban oasis called Huntington Park which was named for Collis Huntington, one of the "Big Four" magnates that included Charles Crocker, Mark Hopkins, and Leland Stanford, founder of Stanford University. They gained their extreme wealth through their control of the Southern Pacific Railroad. The towered Second Empire extravaganza at the left, the home of Charles Crocker, reputedly cost in excess of $2,300,000 to build; it was also destroyed in 1906. Today this block is the site of Grace Cathedral.

10. James Flood mansion on Nob Hill, San Francisco (1885–1886). Designed by architect Augustus Laver for Comstock-silver king James Flood, this great house was built of the reddish-brown sandstone (often called "brownstone") that was especially popular in the East at this time. It is a rather late example of the Italianate style, having quoined corners and heavily hooded windows below a balustraded roofline. Square towers were customarily part of the vocabulary of Victorian Italianate "villas," but they were usually taller than this example. The multi-columned portico is particularly imposing.

12

figure in the development of the early port, and even more than the first alcalde has been credited as one of the true founders of the San Francisco of the future.

Like many who came after him, Richardson's attraction to the area and its residents was sufficient to make him petition the governor for the status of a permanent resident. While settlement by foreigners was officially illegal, the governor realized that Richardson's obvious skills would be valuable to the fledgling port. Richardson soon converted to Catholicism and married María Antonia Martínez, daughter of the Presidio commander Ignacio Martínez. By 1830, Richardson had become a naturalized Mexican citizen. An ex-whaler, he knew much about boats and their construction, and built a launch with which to navigate and survey the Bay, thereby inaugurating San Francisco's shipbuilding industry.

Richardson was also one of the first foreign settlers to construct a significant private dwelling in the new village of Yerba Buena. After camping in a tent on a lot of his choice, he was finally able to secure the land legally. Uphill from the shoreline of the Bay, close to the present-day corner of Clay Street and Grant (then Dupont) Avenue, he first built a small American-style wood-frame house. It wasn't long before other non-Spanish settlers arrived in town and built their own homes nearby.

Richardson soon decided to replace his frame house with a more substantial one constructed with adobe bricks. The one-and-one-half-story home was dubbed La Casa Grande (the big house). Although this was built as a family residence, its function was to be rapidly expanded, making it an important center of civic activities, including a part-time trading post, town-meeting hall, courtroom, and the location of the first Protestant services in the city. At the time of his death in 1856, Richardson was one of the most respected men of his time. High standards were set for the community's future by his vitality, foresight, enterprising nature, and civic pride.

With the establishment of a town government, the beginnings of a working waterfront and residential construction, Yerba Buena was poised on the brink of greater things. Early visitors to the port were drawn to its business, social, and personal opportunities for advancement. It was not unusual for Yankees to marry into Spanish-descended Californio families, so there was a rapid assimilation of new ideas of culture and government that would soon foster more sweeping change.

The first official streets of San Francisco weren't laid out until 1839; obviously, it would take years for the City's architecture to reflect its future reputation. By 1841, there were about thirty families living in the village of Yerba Buena. By 1845, the town had grown to twice its original size, this time extending as far as Sutter, Stockton, and Green Streets, with Montgomery Street parallel to the Bay. The local newspaper the *Star* estimated in 1847 that the town would grow by three to five hundred houses in that year alone. In January 1847, San Francisco became the City's official name.

THE FIGHT FOR CALIFORNIA

California in the 1840s had become something of a political football, for the question of which nation would ultimately possess it had become a matter of increasing concern to the United States. The obvious fear was that it would be taken over by a foreign nation, and thus seriously compromise American security, as well as future expansion. In 1841, President Andrew Jackson's administration, with the consent of Congress, prepared a proposal to purchase the northern half of California from Mexico for half a million dollars. America was on edge about military movements by British and French warships that had been detected off the west coast of South America, and Mexico was powerless to defend California in the event of an invasion.

The mid-1840s saw a rise in California immigration that tipped the balance away from the Mexican Californios. The majority of the immigrants were American settlers, most of whom lived relatively peacefully under Mexican colonial rule. Some, however, who lived in fringe areas were less inclined to submit to it, and opposition to Mexican authority was brewing.

In 1846, John C. Frémont, a captain of topographical engineers for the United States Army, was so impressed by California's majestic beauty that he wrote about it in his memoirs. At the conclusion of a vivid description of the dramatically narrow entry to San Francisco Bay, he bestowed it with the name Chrysopolae or Golden Gate.

Frémont became widely known after a controversy with Governor José Castro's Monterey government. Castro had become concerned about Frémont's questionable intentions, for he was leading an exploratory mission of about sixty guides, surveyors, and helpers through central California. When Frémont received Mexican orders restricting his party's movements and ordering him to leave the province, he disobeyed. This behavior was perceived by Castro as anti-Mexican espionage and considered an act of war. Although it has never been confirmed, it has been thought that President James Polk's administration had been somehow involved in the matter.

Agitated by Frémont's predicament and by what they considered a threat of attack by the Mexican Army, a small band of renegade Americans took the law into their own hands. After successfully rounding up a herd of Mexican horses, they "captured" on June 14, 1846, the town of Sonoma, the site of the northernmost Franciscan mission. In what has been called the Bear Flag Revolt (inspired by its flag's design of a grizzly bear), the band of thirty-three men confronted the town's leader General Mariano G. Vallejo at his home, arrested him, and proclaimed their intention to seize control of the town and its government.

Vallejo, a gracious man who had always gotten along well with the Yankee settlers, defused the potentially violent situation by negotiating peacefully over brandy with the group's leaders. The general and his brother-in-law Jacob Leese, a Yankee from Ohio who had married Vallejo's sister, were taken temporarily under guard to Sutter's Fort near Sacramento, and the formation of a republican government in Sonoma was announced.

Ironically, war between the United States and Mexico had already broken out less than a month before the Bear Flag Revolt; by the following month, the American flag was flying over Monterey after a peaceful takeover by troops under Commodore John D. Sloat, commander of United States ships in the Pacific. Sloat realized that California could be taken without much of a fight, but conflict erupted when Spanish Californians became angered by the coup. Because they fought back with considerable force that caught the Americans by surprise, Sloat turned strategic command of the ensuing battles over to Commodore Robert F. Stockton, who then appointed none other than John C. Frémont to be second in command.

Galvanized by support from the Bear Flaggers and other settlers, troops were sent to southern California, where they were finally successful with little loss of life. On February 2, 1848, the Treaty of Guadalupe Hidalgo was signed, thus ending the Mexican War and formally conceding California to the United States.

THE CALIFORNIA GOLD RUSH

On January 24, 1848, a small quantity of gold dust was detected by James Marshall in a waterway or race that had just been excavated for a new sawmill, the construction of which he had supervised for its owner, Captain Johann August (John) Sutter (a Swiss who had come to Monterey in 1839). It was located in Coloma on the south fork of the American River, about forty-five miles northeast of Sutter's main center of operations, known as Sutter's Fort, a self-styled frontier bastion from which he operated several enterprises including a bakery, mill, blanket factory, and other workshops producing supplies for new settlers. Sutter had obtained a land grant in the Sacramento Valley, where dreams of his own private empire were then realized. He also raised cattle and horses, and farmed wheat on his surrounding land. He acquired a small launch, and because San Francisco was reachable by way of the Sacramento River, it provided another market for his goods.

The discovery of gold on his property gave Sutter much concern about the loyalty of his work force, which was essential for his continued success. He tried in vain to suppress news of the discovery. The land on which the mill was constructed belonged to local Native Americans; he learned from Governor Richard B. Mason that they were unable to cede the property legally. Meanwhile, the secret of the discovery could not be kept quiet, and inevitably many of his workmen left him. Sutter's life would never be the same, and in many ways the Gold Rush was his downfall.

It wasn't until May that the news about gold reached San Francisco, and it was first considered a hoax. That quickly changed when Sam Brannan strode through the streets waving a bottle of gold dust proclaiming, "Gold! Gold from the American River!" Brannan had an ulterior motive for his bold news, for he was co-owner of a supply store in Sutterville, three miles below Sutter's Fort, and he correctly anticipated a bonanza of new business.

While small amounts of gold had been found before in California, this discovery totally eclipsed all others. In the summer of 1848, men were known to pan eight hundred dollars a day; on a Yuba River sandbar a three-month take was seventy-five thousand dollars. Wild stories helped the spread of gold mania throughout the country and soon all around the world. By late summer and fall of 1848, an estimated thirty to fifty thousand dollars in gold was being extracted daily. Before the year was out, the total value of the gold found was conservatively estimated at six million (and as much as ten million) dollars, an inconceivably vast sum at the time.

Even the United States government was impressed. To underscore what was happening, Governor Mason sent some fourteen pounds of gold to President Polk in Washington, where it was put on public display in the War Department. Polk mentioned the California phenomenon in his last State of the Union address on December 5, 1848: "The accounts of the abundance of gold are of such an extraordinary character as would scarcely command belief were they not corroborated by the authentic reports of officers in the public service." Newspapers enthusiastically proclaimed that the "El Dorado of the old Spaniards" had finally been discovered.

The discovery of gold hastened the accomplishment of statehood for California. Its first state legislature was ratified on November 13, 1849, and it was admitted to the Union as a free state by the signature of President Millard Fillmore on September 9, 1850.

THE CITY OF GOLD

San Francisco became host to the world as a result of the Gold Rush. In the first half of 1849, ten thousand so-called Forty-niners sailed into Yerba Buena Cove to prospect for a fast fortune. The number rose quickly to four thousand arriving monthly during the last half of that famous year. The peak year for Gold Rush arrivals occurred in 1852, when nearly sixty-seven thousand landed along the Embarcadero, San Francisco's waterfront thoroughfare.

Wharves were extended as fast as they could be built out into the Bay to accept the multitude of arriving ships; before long the harbor became clogged with far more ships than it could handle, and many of these were abandoned by their captains and crews for the sake of gold.

The scores of abandoned ships that remained in reasonably good condition were transformed into stores, warehouses, saloons, and hotels. One became a church and another a jail.

11. Nob Hill after the earthquake and fire in San Francisco (1906). The extent of the devastation in San Francisco on April 18, 1906, is all too evident in this photograph. The few steel or masonry buildings that remained were reduced to their supporting walls. Looking southeast from Clay Street, the reader can see the remains of the Flood mansion (showing its rear north portico and west side) across the street from the Fairmont Hotel (facing Mason Street between Sacramento and California). Visible downhill to the left are some of the burned-out office buildings of the financial district. Begun in 1902, the Fairmont Hotel was nearly completed at the time of the conflagration. Still structurally sound, it was completely reconstructed within its existing walls.

12. The Pacific Union Club (formerly the James Flood mansion) in San Francisco (reconstructed 1908–1910). After the earthquake and fire of 1906 destroyed the mansion, what remained was purchased by the exclusive Pacific Union Club as their new site. The club chose local architect Willis Polk, who masterfully adapted the house to its new use and retained its aesthetic integrity. His major exterior change was the addition of a pair of single-storey side wings with gracefully rounded ends. Careful matching of material and detailing ensured a seamless blending of old and new. The original cast bronze fence (and a pair of beautiful gates, at the rear) survives in fine condition.

Burning of Cliff House   Ruins of Cliff House

13. Postcard view: The Cliff House, with insets of its burning and in ruins (1907). One of San Francisco's most beloved and popular landmarks, this version of the Cliff House was opened in 1896 by its owner Adolph Sutro. Although it survived the 1906 earthquake with minimal damage, it burned to the ground the following year. Ironically, only two years earlier, the previous Cliff House, which Sutro had owned since the 1880s, had also burned. Reportedly costing $75,000 to build and furnish, this version instantly became the most famous landmark on the northern California coast. Towering eight stories tall, the upper observatory put visitors about 200 feet above the ocean. A must attraction on almost every visitor's list of local sights, it was visited by President William McKinley in 1901, and President Theodore Roosevelt in 1903.

14. The Old United States Mint in San Francisco (1870). Inasmuch as it was one of the few downtown survivors of the 1906 earthquake and fire, this building's structural integrity is undeniably impressive. The unadorned restraint of this design by A. B. Mullett, who specialized in government buildings, is quite typical of the Greek Revival style. The Old Mint was originally the repository of vast quantities of gold and much of the silver from the Comstock Lode.

15. The Old State Capitol Building in Benicia, California (1852–1853). After vying with San Jose and Vallejo as a site for the new state capital of California, the small town of Benicia was, for a brief time, accorded that honor. Named after the wife of General Mariano Vallejo of Sonoma, Benicia was founded in 1846; shortly thereafter it came under consideration to be the Capital, and this building was the result. Designed by Ridder and Houghton of San Francisco, it is possibly the finest surviving example of the Greek Revival style in the state. With simple but elegant detailing and fine proportions, there is a dignified plainness in the soft red brick of its temple front, and the monumental fluted Doric columns of the portico create a satisfying composition of dark and light. Restored in the mid-1950s, the Old State Capitol Building is open to the public.

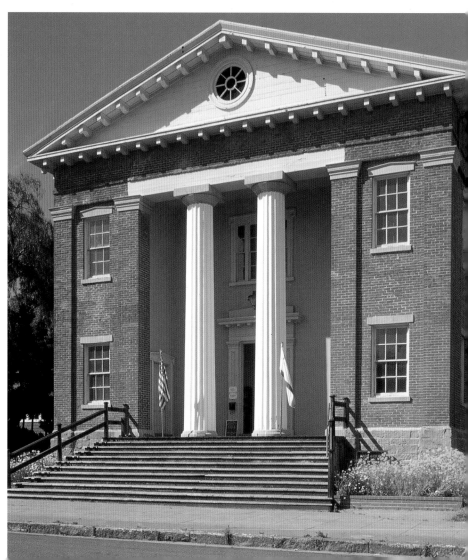

It also happened that other buildings were built alongside some of the landlocked ships that became moored in landfill.

One of the astonishing results of the Gold Rush was that laundry was known to be sent out of the country for washing, sometimes to Hawaii and even as far as China for want of enough local laundresses. New housing was constructed at a record pace, with shiploads of redwood from Mendocino unable to keep up with the demand. The early housing consisted of the simplest frame construction, often with board-and-batten siding, and sometimes only canvas-lined walls for want of anyone to do plastering. Particularly unpleasant visitors were fleas and the innumerable giant Norwegian wharf rats that infested the City from many of the foreign ships moored there.

Serious problems occurred as a result of a free-wheeling lawlessness. As City services were severely taxed, public drunkenness, street fighting, and murder raged out of control. Especially notorious were the Sydney Ducks, a loose group of ex-convicts from Australia who terrorized the town from a rough quarter called Sydney Town. It was in the infamous section called the Barbary Coast, where the unwitting could be drugged and shanghaied for sea duty, with some never to be seen or heard from again.

The problem of rampant crime in early San Francisco was first addressed by vigilante groups of angry citizens who were simply fed up with the terrorizing of the streets. The power and maneuverings of these vigilantes were part of the growing pains of a young city that was simply forced to grow up too quickly.

Because much of it was (and still is) built with lightweight wood-frame construction, the threat of fire has plagued San Francisco throughout its history. Without an organized, city-funded firefighting force, several groups of skilled volunteer companies came to the rescue after enormous fires devastated huge tracts of the city's business and residential districts. The worst of these early fires occurred in May 1851, when sixteen square blocks and almost two thousand buildings were destroyed. Not until the earthquake and fire of 1906 would such a cataclysmic disaster be repeated.

Obviously, all was not chaos and catastrophe in the decades following the Gold Rush. What was consistent, however, was the diversity of the population that caused it to be described as a modern Babel as early as 1849. There was also an early sense of civic pride that grew out of the rapid spurts of growth and rebuilding, which allowed the City to reinvent itself a few times along the way, each time endeavoring to improve itself for its citizens. As a direct result of the fires in the city center, it soon proved necessary for public buildings to be constructed more substantially with brick, stone, and cast iron. Some of these buildings still survive in the vicinity of the Jackson Square Historic District between downtown and North Beach in the neighborhood of what used to be the Barbary Coast.

SAN FRANCISCO'S DOMESTIC ARCHITECTURE

As is true of most large cities, San Francisco's houses have always expressed the great diversity of the tastes and pocketbooks of its citizens. Virtually nothing of the earliest homes remains, but it is possible to visualize the old town by studying paintings, drawings, engravings, and photographs of the period. These images speak to us in hushed tones about a vanished city and inspire us to appreciate the wonderful architecture that remains intact. The succession of San Francisco's fascinating architectural styles is fully discussed and illustrated in detail in the following chapters. The styles encompassed are Gothic Revival, Italianate, Second Empire, Stick/Eastlake, Queen Anne, Colonial Revival/Classical Revival, Hybrid, and those of the Edwardian Era.

VICTORIAN CITY AMUSEMENTS

For amusement during the Victorian era, San Franciscans always enjoyed promenading, people-watching and relaxing, and there were several favorite places for doing so. Among them was the great Palace Hotel, for many years one of the world's best, and certainly the finest hotel west of the Mississippi (if not in the entire country). With a façade bristling with bay windows, the interior boasted a magnificent open rotunda ringed by successive open hallways of the guest floors, and crowned by an iron and glass skylight. The rotunda functioned as the hotel's main entrance and carriage turnaround, and was long the site of the City's most glittering and extravagant social events. It was destroyed in the 1906 disaster.

The Cliff House, a restaurant and bar overlooking Seal Rocks and Ocean Beach, was a favorite Victorian destination for a Sunday excursion after a carriage ride through Golden Gate Park. There have been four incarnations of the Cliff House. The first, a modest hipped-roof structure, was built in 1863, and became an immediate success. The second, an enlargement of the first building to three times its original size, was completed in 1868, but destroyed by fire in 1894. The third and most celebrated Cliff House, built in 1896, was an enormous pile in the so-called Châteauesque style. It became one of the most imposing sights on the California coast until destroyed by a spectacular fire in 1907. The fourth Cliff House was built in 1909 and designed to be less obtrusive on the landscape. It has suffered many remodelings and additions, and it is slated for a major restoration.

Sutro Baths, constructed in the mid-1890s just uphill from the Cliff House, began as a popular public-bathing establishment containing an impressive series of enormous glass-covered swimming pools. It was initially developed by a former mayor, Adolph Sutro, whose name is also attached to nearby Sutro Heights, the present public park located on the rise of land just above the Cliff House. Sutro Heights was the

16. The Children's House in Golden Gate Park, San Francisco (1885). A rare local example of the Romanesque Revival style, this charming public building has a human scale comparable to the private homes built in the same architectural style elsewhere in America. Sometimes called Richardsonian Romanesque, this style was strongly associated with the work of Henry Hobson Richardson, one of the country's most distinguished and influential architects of the nineteenth century. More frequently used for large public or commercial buildings (a good example is Burnham and Root's 1892 Mills Building at Bush and Montgomery Streets in downtown San Francisco), it was considered as being more progressive than other Victorian styles. This building shows many textbook characteristics of the style: a predominant horizontality and massive, ground-hugging presence; the use of large, roughly finished stone blocks for color and texture; rounded Roman arches and shadowy arcades, integral architectural sculpture in the detailing, and an eyebrow dormer situated behind a gable. Designed by the firm of Percy and Hamilton, it was constructed with funds bequeathed by the estate of Senator William Sharon, one of the Comstock silver magnates. Currently used as studio space for art classes, it was part of an early park complex dedicated to children that included a playground and a magnificent carousel that was recently restored.

17. Detail of the front-entry arcade of the Children's House. Deeply shadowed front porches like this were typical of Romanesque Revival buildings. It was on Romanesque column capitals and broad rounded arches above entrance doorways that sculpture was usually found, sometimes including faces and creatures that are woven into the tendrils and leaves of stylized vegetation.

site of his private estate until a fire destroyed his home there, and the property was later given to the City for use as a park. The concept of Sutro Baths was copied in other cities and reflected a popular Victorian pastime that combined healthy exercise with socializing.

As the public changed their use of leisure time such places fell out of fashion. By the 1960s, the swimming pools at Sutro Baths had long been closed off, and an attempt at adaptive reuse of the structure had converted the largest pool into an indoor skating rink. The rest of the building had evolved into a rather shopworn tourist attraction that drew from a still steady stream of visitors to the Cliff House. It was destroyed by fire in 1966.

THE BAY AREA LANDSCAPE

The splendor of the San Francisco Bay Area landscape contributes to the allure that has continually drawn so many here. In what may be the most spectacular meeting of land and sea cradling any large metropolitan area, it is the region's striking topography that has perhaps been its most compelling asset. It is not necessary to go far to be entranced by its beauty. The sometimes almost improbable siting of San Francisco up and down multiple hills has created a collection of stunning urban vistas. While most of its natural topography has been covered with buildings and its steep hills overlaid with a surprisingly rigid street grid, a glimpse of shimmering water or a distant mountain view may be literally just around the corner or at the end of the block. While some visitors are quite happy never to leave the City's reaches, there are entirely different worlds to explore across the Bay or down the peninsula that put even more magnificence of the natural world within easy reach.

From the highest Bay Area mountaintops, clear days can provide sweeping outlooks extending far inland across the Central Valley to the Sierra Nevada mountains. Most of the region's loftiest promontories are on public land and are fully hikeable by hardy souls. Beneath these, the rolling slopes and gentle folds of distinctively rounded grassy hills are made a vivid green by the winter rains, or baked to a golden-brown by the sun of rainless summers. Punctuating their contours are clumps of deep-green native oaks, seemingly pruned to a picturesque perfection. In some places, one finds striking compositions formed by groups of boulders entwined with the oaks.

There is a spiritual hush that envelops the tantalizing cool and moist redwood forest that evokes a sense of the primeval past. One of the most accessible and visited forests is Muir Woods, which amazingly lies only about a dozen miles north of bustling San Francisco. Northern California's coastline changes strikingly from a smoothly horizontal sweep of sandy beach to vertical rocky cliffs that plunge into the churning surf. Despite continuous development, the Bay Area remains, almost everywhere, a region where Nature seems ever present.

THE BAY AREA'S FAMOUS FAULTS

Beguiling as many find the scenery, a disturbing aspect of the Bay Area's geography can be described as the restless heart of Mother Nature beating deep underground. While most visitors are generally aware of the constant potential for an earthquake, few actually specifically avoid the area because of it. Perhaps this undercurrent of danger even adds a frisson of excitement for some. Most residents prefer not to dwell on the fact that they are living in one of the most seismically active areas of the world because of the multiple fault lines that run through the Bay Area. They are certainly aware that this constitutes an ever-present risk, but relatively few who have made their homes here have fled, or would flee, for that reason alone. The wooden Victorian houses that remain standing today in San Francisco form a remarkable collective testimony to the structural resilience and durability of the native redwood with which most were built. In the Bay Area's famous earthquake disaster of 1906, the buildings that were most damaged or destroyed had been built on filled land that was either once the shallow edges of the bay, swampy marshland, or perhaps a filled-in creekbed. It was the insubstantial nature of the ground beneath them, rather than inherent structural weakness, that caused the most destruction.

The vast majority of the most devastating damage of 1906 was due to the fires that raged out of control for days. Also, sufficient water was unavailable to fight the fires because the water mains had been destroyed by the earthquake. While San Francisco's downtown and adjoining industrial districts as well as nearby residential areas were utterly decimated, the balance of other populated zones were largely spared. It is these neighborhoods that comprise the most complete groups of surviving Victorian houses, the treasures of present-day San Francisco.

LEARNING FROM OLD HOUSES

For those of us longing to learn more about the past, old buildings are an important source of information. Many of us have experienced a compelling connection to the past simply by walking through the front door of an old house and savoring the intangible atmosphere of its interiors. Although the interpretive displays and docent tours that are common to most house museums can make much easier the process of learning about a historic home, a private house doesn't yield its secrets so easily.

However, the new owner of an architecturally significant landmark home will generally have an easier time learning about its history than would the new owner of a humble cottage, for the grander house would invariably be the subject of greater local interest. In either case, if information is not available from a previous owner, a potential resource could be the local historical society. If the house is located in a designated historic district or has been featured on a house tour, it may be that basic facts, like the construction date or the architect's name, may have already been researched and documented.

One of the first places to start searching for more information about a particular house is to take the time to consult available city records. Obtaining copies of the records and keeping a house-history file is a good idea that will also benefit future owners. Building and water department records, as well as city directories of the period, frequently yield names, dates, and sometimes other facts that could encourage further exploration. Armed with a list of names, it is sometimes possible to locate surviving members of the families of previous owners, which can occasionally result in access to period photographs or sometimes interesting verbal histories or odd anecdotes about the house. For a fee, it is sometimes possible to locate individuals in the communities who are already highly skilled at researching house histories.

If we are willing to "listen," old houses have much to tell us about their past history. For example, the configuration of the floor plans and various room appointments can inform us about the prevailing social customs of early occupants. Trends in the popular culture of over a century ago can be revealed in the form, motifs, or details of intact woodwork elements, plaster ornaments, or rare surviving interior finishes, such as wallpaper or stenciling. Each successive layer of old wallpaper tells us something about popular styles of different periods, and can also inform us about the taste and budget of the household that selected it.

We can even glean fascinating tidbits about the personal habits, hobbies, or family rituals of previous occupants by closely inspecting the areas of old houses less subject to redecoration or remodeling. Attics, cellars or basements, storerooms, or even closets might have a few traces of past activities that could (literally) include handwriting on the wall. It is not uncommon to find the marks and measurements documenting the growth of children. Later structural alterations are an intrinsic part of a building's story; just because they aren't original features, they shouldn't necessarily be reversed.

IN SEARCH OF OLD HOUSES

Reflecting a trend that is increasingly common across the country, many Bay Area communities stage annual house tours, usually as benefits for historical societies, neighborhood groups, or local preservation associations, and most occur in the spring or fall. While it can be tempting to drive around to cover more territory quickly, it is advisable to park the car as soon as a promising area has been found. Because they are loaded with details that are sometimes quite small in scale, it is much better to observe Victorian houses slowly and on foot. Most of San Francisco, and much of its immediate environs, are sympathetically geared toward exploration by walking. When armed with even a modest bit of knowledge about Victorian architecture, such as we have tried to provide in this book, a neophyte old-house watcher will find the experience greatly enhanced, and some may be moved to pursue their budding connoisseurship further. Because it is interactive and ever-changing, the observation of old houses is a particularly satisfying pursuit, made even more enjoyable in the company of others who share the same interest.

Victorian House Planning
Solutions to Nineteenth-Century Housing Needs

SUBDIVIDING THE VICTORIAN CITY

The need for the dense, wall-to-wall siting of many houses in San Francisco grew out of the high value placed on the land early in its history. Its survey and division into buildable lots were already underway before the Gold Rush. The first rather crude map of 1839 drawn by Jean Jacques Vioget began this process. It was refined and expanded in 1847 by the newly appointed City surveyor Jasper O'Farrell, a civil engineer from Ireland, well-qualified by reason of his previous post of surveyor general of Alta California under the Mexican government.

Continuing the orientation of the street grid established by Vioget, O'Farrell's survey expanded San Francisco's plotted area to about eight hundred acres; its boundaries were extended north to Francisco Street, south to Post Street, east to beyond Market Street, and west to Leavenworth Street. Reflected in this survey was the "O'Farrell Swing," a necessary two-degree correction in the angle of the street grid of Vioget's first plan.

O'Farrell's survey established much of the future character of San Francisco's street grid through his bold plotting of Market Street, which was destined to become one of the City's primary thoroughfares. Departing from the older grid, and with a strong diagonal axis, it was aligned with a westerly view of Twin Peaks, and it made a direct connection from the developing downtown area toward the vicinity of Mission Dolores. As a result of its departure from the right-angle orientation, Market Street created a series of irregular, triangulated flatiron-shape intersections on its north side where it abutted the existing street grid. In contrast, the newer blocks laid out on the south side of Market were set at right angles to the new thoroughfare, and these were of significantly larger size than those previously established to the north. Differences in block sizes, as well as Market Street's diagonal axis, impeded direct crossings between the two sides of town. While not immediate, this arrangement created future traffic-flow problems, that to some extent have persisted to the present.

Within a year, the street grid north of Market was extended to Front Street near the waterfront, and Larkin Street on the west; across Market, it reached to Townsend Street on the south, and Ninth Street to the west. This expansion reflected the phenomenal growth experienced by the area. In 1851, another survey was made by William Eddy, who succeeded O'Farrell as the City's surveyor. He expanded its official map, plotting most of the newer blocks in the area south of Market and west of Ninth (then called Johnston) Street, where the direction of the grid turns in the direction of Mission Dolores. It is notable that many lots surveyed on the outer fringes of both O'Farrell's and Eddy's plans were under water or in marshy areas, but were planned as being buildable once they could receive landfill. In fact, because of their potential as sites for shipping commerce, some of those lots still submerged would actually become the most highly valued.

Another permanent result of O'Farrell's survey was the selection of street names, most of which commemorated those prominent in the development of California both before and after its American possession. Along with those of pioneer residents Bryant, Brannan, Folsom, Harrison, Leavenworth, and Hyde, the names of O'Farrell and Eddy assumed their place on City street signs. The names of United States military officers Dupont, Frémont, Jones, Kearney, Montgomery, and Taylor also became familiar local addresses. Although quite a few have since been changed to honor others who came later, many of San Francisco's street names have a curious story or bit of local legend behind them, which further enhances one's sense of the early City (a 1984 book by Louis K. Lowenstein called *Streets of San Francisco* covers this topic thoroughly).

The sale of lots by the City became a viable means for the financing of necessary public works, such as street maintenance or various government services. Under both O'Farrell and Eddy's surveys, the proportions of San Francisco's city blocks continued to be based on incremental divisions that were multiples of the "Spanish yard," or *vara* (approximately $33\frac{1}{3}$ inches), continuing the precedent set by Vioget's plan of 1839. Each block in the north of Market Street vicinity consisted of six lot divisions, each of which was fifty *varas* square. From these, further subdivisions were made by developers to

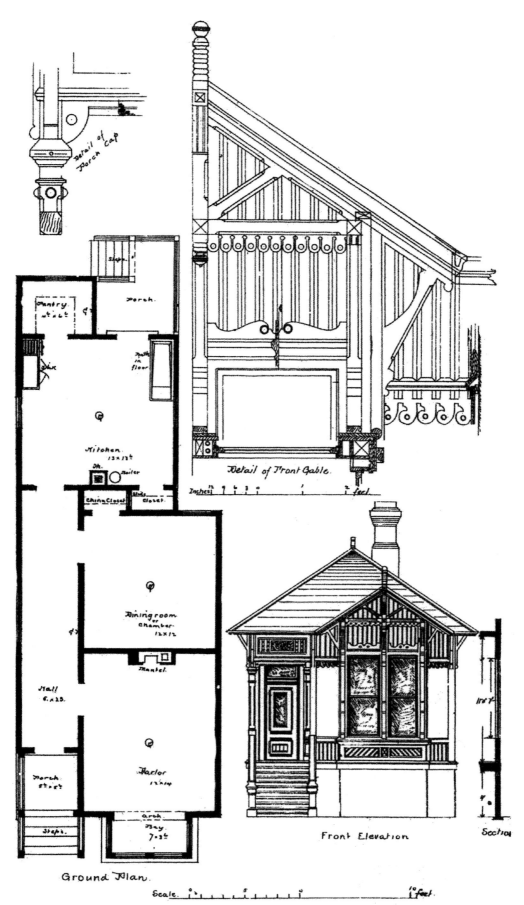

Detail of Porch Cap.

Detail of Front Gable.

Inches 12 9 6 3 0   1   2 feet

Steps.

Pantry
6x6½

Sink.

Porch.

Bath
in
floor

Kitchen
13x13½

Sh.   Boiler

China Closet   Store
Closet.

Dining room
or
chamber
12x12

Mantel.

Hall
6x25.

Parlor
12x14

Porch
6x6½

Arch
Bay
7x3½

Steps.

Ground Plan.

Front Elevation.

Section.

Scale.   0   5   10 feet

S & J. C. Newsom. Architects.
504 Kearny St.
San Francisco. Cal.

18. Floor plan, front elevation, and detail drawings for a working-class cottage (1884). This modestly scaled design was included in *Picturesque California Homes*, an 1884 pattern book published by San Francisco architects Samuel and Joseph Cather Newsom. This house, of about 700 square feet, was the smallest in the book. In comparison to the others, it also had the cheapest per-square-foot price; its "cost complete" was $700.

To minimize labor and material costs, the choice of the Stick/Eastlake style for the façade made sense, for with few lathe-turned elements, it required only the simplest cuts of wood for its exterior detailing. Elements of the style seen here on the larger details of the front gable and a porch post are the beveled or chamfered edges of the roof brackets, the upper gable's open truss work, panelized insets of simple linear vertical and diagonal patterns for surface interest, and the outlines of flat, fretsawn embellishments adding a few curves.

With its eighteen-foot width and bracketed roof overhangs projecting almost two feet on either side, this house could fit a standard-size twenty-five-foot-wide lot. Its hipped roof contributes scale and more street presence than a flat one, but the primary design statement of this façade is made by the ornamented gable above a projecting bay window. Raised up four feet from ground level, the front door is reached by a few steps alongside the bay window.

The entry opens into a long hall (of twenty-five feet), and if the doorway to the kitchen at its far end was open, the sightline would be extended to as much as forty-three feet through both the kitchen and pantry. Along with economy of space, an important design goal for small houses was to maximize their feeling of space. The Victorian planning ideal of a distinct separation between rooms and their functions, combined with a narrow city lot, encouraged the need for such long hallways. Adherence to this convention precluded the more spacious feeling that could be achieved in small houses by incorporating instead the square footage and circulation function of these long hallways into public rooms. This effective small-house-planning innovation would set early twentieth-century bungalows apart from their Victorian predecessors.

However, a surprisingly practical consideration seen here is the generous five-foot width indicated for the hall, which adds the potential of greater utility to an otherwise mere circulation space. By adding extra width, halls could be made to work harder and easily accommodate a hall stand and other practical pieces, like a bookcase, chest of drawers, a small wardrobe (or other storage cabinets), and perhaps some extra side chairs to supplement dining-room or parlor seating.

No matter what the household budget would permit, the front parlor received the most attention to decoration and furnishings. In a small house the parlor's functions were many: it was the place to receive and entertain visitors, the place for the family to spend leisure time together, and potentially a private, quiet space for study or reading. (Then as now, most of a household's activity centered around the kitchen.) The symmetrical shape of this plan's parlor with the fireplace mantel on axis with the bay window, anticipates the balanced placement of a parlor suite, typically consisting of a settee, two armchairs, and two or four side chairs. Other furnishings might have included a center table, side or lamp tables, a secretary or desk, and possibly an upright piano. The bay window would be a good spot for a few potted plants, and for daytime reading, a chair with a footstool.

Because this house has no designated bedrooms, the plan implies the alternate use of the dining room as a bedroom. Such limited space

dictated that even the kitchen might have alternate uses; there would be no space left unused.

When modest dwellings like this one were designed with no separate bathroom facilities, a bathtub was often located in the kitchen. In lieu of any indoor toilet, chamber pots or an outside privy were used. While none is indicated here, many back porches were fitted with more convenient pull-chain flush toilets.

Alongside the kitchen, for more light and ventilation, a narrow set-back about four feet wide permits a side window there and allows a rear-facing window in the dining room. Between the kitchen and dining room, a closet is connected by a slide or pass-through to an adjoining dining room china closet, most likely fitted with a built-in sideboard for serving and storage. The placement of the kitchen's second window on the left side suggests that it opened onto a narrow walkway alongside the house. A third window in the pantry is an additional source of light and air. A covered rear porch provided access to a yard, as well as a place to dry laundry in wet weather.

maximize the potential returns on their investment. Today, many City-lot dimensions still reflect their early division based on the Spanish *vara*.

Some of the waterfront land that had been reserved for use by the Federal Government was freed up for public ownership at an 1847 auction; prices averaged between $50 and $100, for a lot measuring $15\frac{1}{2}$ *varas* wide by fifty *varas* deep (approximately forty-three feet wide by $137\frac{1}{2}$ feet deep). Foreshadowing a phenomenon of more recent years, these early lots would prove shrewd investments for their new owners; in only a year or two, immediately following the onset of the Gold Rush, these same lots were able to fetch more than a hundred times their original cost.

If its space was exploited to the maximum, a city block could yield as many as thirty-eight residential lots. In the early days, supply and demand had much to do with determining what was an acceptable or so-called standard lot size. However, after further development, and through comparison to other dense urban centers such as New York, it was eventually determined that the most typical width of a residential lot in San Francisco would be twenty-five feet (compared to New York's average of only seventeen feet). Still, many variations would occur.

Depths of San Francisco's residential lots could vary considerably. Some were as shallow as sixty-five feet, while the deepest lots were close to one hundred forty feet; however, most averaged between ninety and one hundred twenty feet. One determining factor for lot depth was if the rear boundary intersected with a neighboring lot that fronted on another side of the block. An abbreviated depth often resulted when a lot was close to a corner.

For those who could afford it, more spacious building lots could be created by combining more than one parcel. Although some have since reverted to smaller sizes, some expanded lots were originally large enough to accommodate an additional outbuilding or two; carriage houses, stables, water towers, chickenhouses, or even small barns were not

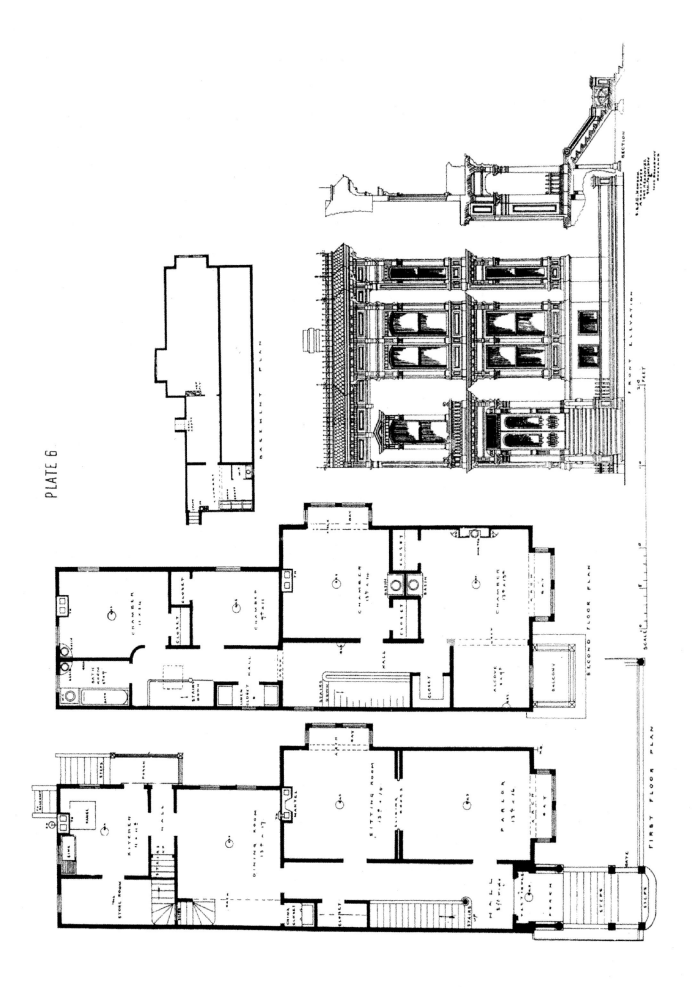

PLATE 6

BASEMENT PLAN

FRONT ELEVATION

SECOND FLOOR PLAN

FIRST FLOOR PLAN

19. Floor plans, front elevation, and section drawing for a middle-class row house (1884). Reproduced from *Picturesque California Homes*, this house embodies a classic San Francisco row-house formula that was repeated in great numbers as either single-family or two-flat buildings, and its general appearance resembles many examples photographed for this book. Architects Samuel and Joseph Cather Newsom were Canadians, but they moved to San Francisco soon after 1860, and they are now considered two of California's most important Victorian-era architects.

The estimated costs of the house plans ranged from $700 to $15,000, with the average cost being about $4,700. The "cost complete" for this house was listed at $4,500. This is one of this pattern book's nineteen plans with a documented location: it was built as the "C. Evans" residence on a corner lot at 22nd and Capp Streets in the Mission District.

While most of the Newsoms' designs in the book were lively, inventive examples of predominantly Queen Anne and hybrid styles, this was one of their more conservative efforts. Still a hybrid, it is a restrained blending of the Stick/Eastlake style with some Italianate elements and Second Empire influence. A topping of cast-iron cresting was a popular detail that might be found on any of these styles cited.

Aimed at fulfilling the needs of families in the professional or merchant class, this plan includes most of the popular features that would complete a theoretical checklist of a typical middle-class family of the 1880s. To appeal to those with somewhat higher aspirations, this house was designed for a corner or extra-wide lot (this plan indicates a lot of about thirty-five feet), for it has a projecting bay window on the side designed to match the one on the façade.

The first-floor plan and section drawing shows two steps up to a landing from the street approach, where a garden gate leads to an enclosed front yard. This example shows a variation of a wooden picket fence, but cast-iron fencing was often preferred by those who could afford it. Hillside lots, combined with the results of street grading, sometimes required property fencing to be set on top of a higher retaining wall.

The basement plan shows that only a portion of the rear area was developed into a laundry room. Not accessible from the inside, it required entry from the back yard and also included an extra toilet. Basement functions were usually strictly utilitarian (a coal chute is on the plan), with a variety of storage areas. To compensate for the limits of a shallow lot, some plans utilized basement areas for kitchens, which freed up more of their main living level for family use. Inside access was usually gained by an extension of a rear stairway to the lower level. Alternatively, many houses had inside stairways to their basements beneath their front stairs, which sometimes in grander homes led to a large, versatile ballroom space for entertaining, as well as children's play space. Sometimes houses also had separate servants' quarters in their basement levels. Many basements were later converted into garages. Most garage-door openings on the façades of Victorian houses are not original features.

Lending some grandeur to the entry is a projecting covered portico, characteristic of many such row houses, which allowed the architects to expand on the façade's design statement. Here this was achieved through a repetition of detailing, the pair of imposing free-standing columns to support its roof, and the balustrade enclosing a small balcony.

A vestibule (indicated on the plan) was often created by two sets of front doors: the outer ones were used as a social signal by the occupants; if they were receiving visitors, these would be left open. When closed, they indicated that either no one was at home, or that its occupants were otherwise indisposed. The inner doors, which gave direct entry into the house, were likely to be more ornate and incorporate glass panels to admit daylight into the hall; often etched and cut with decorative designs, these panels might also be fitted with leaded art glass to add color, pattern, and status.

The floor plan of this house demonstrates how, when its occupants could afford it, space was provided for as many of the public and private functions of a Victorian household as possible. For example, the front parlor was reserved for formal occasions, especially for the receiving and entertaining of visitors. Therefore the parlor—together with the first-floor hall and dining room—was given the most impressive decoration the family could afford. Generally used as the family's informal living area, the second or family parlor (or sitting room) connects to the front parlor through a wide opening fitted with sliding pocket doors. Bay windows in each room provide ample light and create additional space. This parlor might also be used as a library, music room, den or study, and possibly an occasional guest room.

Defined by a room-wide arch (indicated on the plan by a dotted line), a dining-room alcove would often house a showy, freestanding sideboard, and a separate built-in china closet is also shown on the plan. On the opposite side beneath the rear staircase, a slide or pass-through is indicated between the dining room and a storeroom off the kitchen. It opens into a corner of the dining room that was probably also fitted with a small, built-in serving cabinet. The room's pair of windows on the side were made possible by the building's offset, which also permitted space off the kitchen for a side porch and steps to the back yard. The generous dimensions of the dining room affirm its central importance in the typical Victorian family's daily life.

The decorative scheme of the first-floor entry hall would likely have continued upstairs, but most often only as far as the front stair hall. A common configuration seen in this plan is the front chamber or bedroom, which features a bay window, fireplace, a sink built into a recess, and a closet. Separated by an archway, an adjoining alcove area was designed to hold the bed. While frequently used for the master bedroom, in some households this entire front area became an upstairs family sitting room. The function of the small balcony above the entry portico, although reachable through a window, was generally more decorative than practical.

In a variation of this plan seen in many otherwise similar houses, the second-floor alcove located over the main stairs was built as a small separate room that opened into the hall, and could be used as a dressing room, a nursery, a sewing room, a study, or an extra bedroom. It has been suggested that such an alcove was intended as a "fainting" room or resting place for visiting ladies to retire to after ascending the long staircase, where they could loosen their corsets and recover their composure on a "fainting couch."

The second of the two largest bedrooms also opens off the front stair hall. Like the front room, it incorporates a bay window, built-in sink, and closet. An alternate arrangement seen in some houses is the use of a connecting door between these two rooms to form a self-contained suite (for more convenience, many houses have been remodeled to fit a second, compact bathroom in the area between the two bedrooms).

Separated from the front by an arched doorway, the back hall leads to a pair of smaller secondary bedrooms usually assigned to children or other family members. The large linen closet and rear stairway are brightened by a skylight indicated by the dotted square, with a fully equipped bathroom at the far end. The rear bedroom's proximity to the bathroom easily allowed for the extra amenity of a corner sink. Then considered a modern innovation, the fashion for sinks in bedrooms had replaced the former standard feature of a washstand with a pitcher and bowl, and somewhat lessened the problem of having only one bathroom.

unusual in more outlying parts of town. Corner lots, considered to be the most valuable, were also the most likely spots where a neighborhood's largest free-standing homes, surrounded by gardens, would be sited for maximum visibility.

From its earliest efforts, local city planning was criticized for the way in which the plotting of its conventional grid of streets completely ignored the sometimes abrupt changes in local topography. In fact, the extreme steepness of streets for some blocks rendered them impassable to horsedrawn vehicles and effectively reduced access to that of staircases in place of sidewalks. While the inaccessibility of many inclines would be transformed by the advent of the cable car in the 1870s, the limited access of some such blocks has persisted to the present.

Objects of much dispute about legal ownership in the early years of the City's development were the remaining undeveloped tracts of land in and around San Francisco (and elsewhere in the Bay Area) that had survived intact as ranchos from the Mexican days. Contributing to a maze of unclear titles on much of these lands were squatters who occupied so-called Pueblo or Outside Lands in the dune-ridden western reaches of the City (many in the vicinity of the future Golden Gate Park). Becoming a hotly debated political issue, disputes over who had the right to clear title to such lands sometimes created violent altercations between opposing sides. The concept of possession as nine-tenths of the law allowed many to retain what may not necessarily have been theirs to keep. In fact, if squatters occupied claimed land for at least five years, and then (after 1878) paid all of the state, county, and municipal tax assessments, they were able to gain legal title to that property.

Because some of these parcels had a barrage of conflicting claims sometimes involving multiple claimants, local lawyers soon made land law a lucrative specialty, with some charging excessive fees—as much as one-half of the total value of the land under contention. Parcels of land that were long held by Spanish-speaking Californio ranchers, but perhaps were lacking in proper documentation, were frequently the targets of greedy newcomers.

The laws that accompanied the establishment of California's statehood helped seal the fate of much disputed land in favor of the Yankees, for in many such cases it was impossible for the longstanding occupants to pay the new property taxes that were demanded of them. Other reasons that a substantial amount of land originally claimed by the Californios ended up on the auction block were due, sadly, to problems agitated by the langauge barrier. Also, since many of the old ranchos were quite self-sufficient, their original settlers were often unable to come up with sufficient "Yankee cash" to cover property taxes that were specified as payable in U.S. coin.

A conspicuous lack of land set aside for public parks in the first surveys of San Francisco was a widely perceived flaw in early city planning. However, as the forlorn, windswept lands further to the west were eyed for future development, a major if momentary shift in this policy resulted in one of the world's greatest urban gardens, Golden Gate Park. Once a dispute with the Federal Government over ownership of this particular land was resolved, resulting legislation paved the way for its clear title to the City in 1868.

Behind the scenes, powerful civic leaders had strong political and opportunistic interests in how such a park would raise property values in the area, much like Central Park had done for the undeveloped uptown reaches of New York—where within five years, they had appreciated by a thousand percent. As the designer of Central Park, Frederick Law Olmstead, America's greatest landscape architect, was initially consulted about the planning of the park, but he was convinced that a lush, English-style, water-intensive park like the one envisioned by those in power was inappropriate if not impossible to realize in such an inhospitable location. Alternately, he recommended the park be sited in a more accessible part of town near the City's center, protected from driving ocean winds, in the vicinity of today's Van Ness Avenue.

Olmsted's recommendations fell on deaf ears. Instead, in 1870, a young civil engineer from Maryland named William Hammon Hall was hired—first, to lead a survey and planting study, and then to oversee the implementation of his design as engineer and superintendent. Over the next several years, Golden Gate Park was laboriously but ingeniously engineered out of what had been a vast wasteland of sand dunes. Larger than Central Park by more than one hundred fifty acres, it comprised a meandering procession of roads and pathways, interspersed with ponds and lakes. Encompassing half a mile in width and three miles in length, it stretched westward from present-day Stanyan Street out to Ocean Beach, and became an immediate popular success.

Famous local horticulturalist John McLaren, the beloved gardener of the Park for fifty-six years, masterfully planted, nurtured, and refined its various features into what is still a masterpiece today. Echoing a continuing controversy, "Uncle John" McLaren was also consistently opposed to what he perceived as the excessive placement of commemorative statues, and the construction of buildings, within Park boundaries.

LAUNCHING THE HOME-BUILDING INDUSTRY

Before issues of design and construction could be considered, the average citizen who wished to build a new home first needed to secure a buildable lot. Two important forces had a great influence on the local building climate that created San Francisco's Victorian houses. One that enabled many average San Francisco citizens to become homeowners was the formation of so-called homestead associations. Not exactly builders or developers, these groups could be best described as subdividers of potential residential property. Organized as private corporations, they purchased large tracts of land, and then solicited others (i.e. future homeowners) to participate in their investment plans.

After an initial fee or deposit was paid, an individual was obligated to make monthly payments (usually about ten dollars) that were credited toward obtaining clear title to a buildable lot. Eventually, some homestead associations did evolve into real-estate developers, expanding their activities beyond merely securing land to include the actual construction of houses. By the end of the 1860s, as many as one hundred seventy homestead associations had been formed in San Francisco. A similar concept was also applied to other land-investment pursuits, particularly agricultural ones, in the surrounding Bay Area.

The other major force that fostered San Francisco's home-building industry was the formation of numerous savings-and-loan organizations. It began with the formation in 1854 of the San Francisco Accumulating Fund Association, which in three years was reorganized as the Savings & Loan Society. This group collected savings deposits, then paid out a monthly dividend to its members, among whom were the City's most prominent and wealthy citizens. Because its elite membership tended to avoid foreign nationalities, other similar savings-and-loan groups emerged to address the financial needs of the City's various ethnic communities.

In 1859, the Hibernia Savings and Loan Society was founded to assist the rapidly growing Irish population; within five years it could boast the City's largest number of depositors, as well as the greatest amount of savings. Similar groups were soon developed for the local French, Italian, and German populations as well as other ethnic groups that were likely to be shunned by the American banking institutions. Because of their persistent outsider status during the early years, the Chinese were, by necessity, inclined to be as financially self-sufficient as possible. Fraternal groups such as the Odd Fellows and the Masonic Order formed money-saving organizations for their members. The solid foundation of wealth created here through the early savings-and-loan groups did much to ensure San Francisco's future strength as a leading financial and banking center.

Separate from financial concerns, the physical problems that accompanied housebuilding on terrain as variable as San Francisco's were complex and sometimes expensive to resolve. Because the City's streets blithely ignored so many ups and downs, building sites often needed considerable leveling before construction could begin. Despite the sustained presence of so many of its hills, there was actually far more leveling and grading in San Francisco than is commonly supposed.

Present-day visitors can still see the results of mutilated land not only due to lot and street leveling, but from industries that required quarrying for gravel, digging clay, or crushing rocks for brick, and blasting hillsides for stone ballast. The east side of Telegraph Hill has been unstable for years because of earlier undermining. It wasn't Mother Nature who created the picturesque rocky peak of Corona Heights Park, it was the incessant quarrying by the Gray Brothers' brick factory once sited on its slope.

The ongoing need to move tons of earth and rocks for street and lot leveling went hand-in-hand with another pressing need: landfill to expand the usable waterfront. Over time, the grades of a number of streets were leveled more than once, leaving earlier buildings at a distinct height disadvantage, unless their owners were willing to raise or lower them. This fact might explain the seemingly odd relationships of house to sidewalk in some neighborhoods. Another phenomenon that occurred more often than most would imagine is the moving of houses, usually an effect of hill-leveling projects or site redevelopment that dictated either relocating or demolishing a house.

Another key issue that was closely tied to the development of San Francisco's Victorian houses was the development of various public utilities, most of which began as privately owned and operated businesses. Ample supplies of water and gas (and eventually, electricity) assured steady local growth, and the construction of residential and commercial architecture. Whatever the latest municipal improvements were, San Francisco was not likely to wait long before getting them.

Street lamps illuminated by coal-gas appeared downtown by 1853, when such lighting was also put into use in some hotels and theatres. Within three years, the local gas company could boast in excess of four thousand customers. Foreshadowing the bright future of telecommunications, the once-isolated outpost gained a direct and immediate link to New York via the telegraph in 1862. Even more sweeping were the changes brought about by the Bay Area's transcontinental connection by railroad, completed in 1869, beginning a far more interactive period with the rest of the country. It was after this date that Oakland, the true western railroad terminus across the Bay, began in earnest its ascendancy as a major city, and San Francisco was long to remain a ferry-boat ride away for all visitors arriving by train.

After the railroad arrived, personal travel was much easier and cheaper; suddenly, long-missed relatives could be reunited by a simple train ride. A more important result was improved commerce. For housing, this meant that certain building materials, supplies, and a variety of home furnishings and other products that were previously rare or unavailable (unless locally made) could be ordered, shipped, and delivered. Less than a decade later, another milestone: California's first telephone exchange opened in San Francisco in 1878.

Then as now, not everyone who settled in San Francisco necessarily wanted to build or even own a house. Because of San Francisco's emergence as a business center, the presence of satellite offices of national firms was not unusual, and as a result there was a steady influx of new residents who came here under the auspices of their employers. While most of these new arrivals tended to be upper-middle- to upper-class households, they were just as likely to seek the alternative of rental housing as citizens of lesser means. In fact, the City has traditionally had a significant rental market with a broad socioeconomic range; even today, the majority of San Francisco households comprises renters. Of course, this need

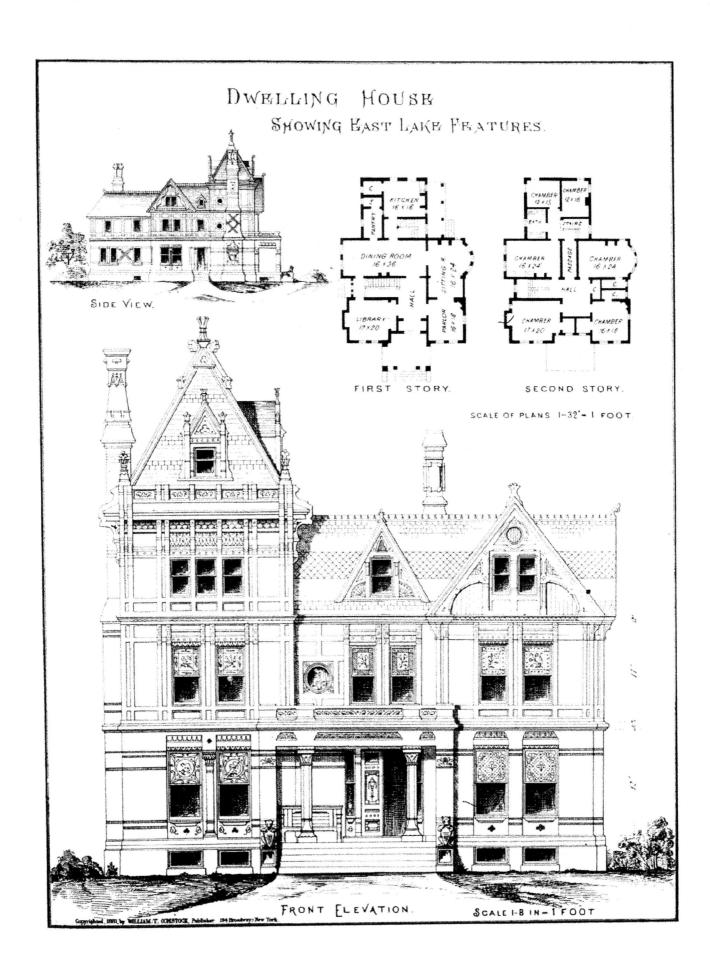

DWELLING HOUSE
SHOWING EAST LAKE FEATURES.

SIDE VIEW.

KITCHEN
16 x 16

PANTRY

C

DINING ROOM
16 x 36

SITTING R.
16 x 24

HALL

LIBRARY
17 x 20

PARLOR
16 x 18

FIRST STORY.

CHAMBER
12 x 15

CHAMBER
12 x 16

BATH

STAIRS

CHAMBER
16 x 24

CHAMBER
16 x 24

PASSAGE

HALL

C.

C.

CHAMBER
17 x 20

CHAMBER
16 x 18

SECOND STORY.

SCALE OF PLANS 1-32" = 1 FOOT.

FRONT ELEVATION.

SCALE 1-8 IN = 1 FOOT.

28

20. Floor plans, with front and side elevation drawings, for an upper-class detached residence (1881). These plans for a "Dwelling House Showing East Lake Features" appeared in a popular pattern book called *Modern Architectural Designs and Details* published in 1881 by William T. Comstock in New York. Not an architect but an architectural editor and publisher, Comstock was a former partner of A. J. Bicknell, who had published similar plan books throughout the 1870s.

Representative of many pattern books that were published on the East Coast but distributed in California and influential there, this book did include one plan for a house "recently erected in California." While not all the architects or locations of the various plans were identified, most were East Coast examples. In addition to house plans, Comstock included commercial store fronts and their interior fittings, as well as some framing plans, and a considerable wealth of interior details.

On the title page, Comstock's pattern book was presented as ". . . showing new and original designs in the Queen Anne, Eastlake, Elizabethan and other modernized styles," which were ". . . adapted to the requirements of seaside and summer resorts, suburban and country places," by "a number of prominent architects of different localities, prepared expressly for this work."

Like this example, most of the designs were for fully detached houses that required much larger lots than what was typical of cities like New York and San Francisco. They were targeted at the middle-to upper-middle-class market seeking to build homes in suburban or country settings where land was much cheaper. Yet, in every major urban area, there remained a small but sufficiently well-to-do clientele who wanted to build dream houses in the heart of their cities. Inspired by the same sort of ambition that brought great success in business, rich Americans were fueled by keen competition with their peers. The great mansions erected on San Francisco's Nob Hill were prime examples of such architectural oneupmanship.

At first, the Stick/Eastlake-style influence on American domestic architecture was a progressive trend influenced by the English Arts and Crafts Movement, with a more honest expression of materials as structural elements and a shift away from historic revivalism. By the date of this house, however, the style's intentions were somewhat muddled and not the progressive force they may have been a decade earlier. The house nevertheless remains a fashion statement evocative of its time. An ambitious composition, the design recalls many of the imposing, freestanding houses built in Victorian San Francisco. Because of this pattern book's wide circulation, it might possibly have inspired some of them; the architects of Nob Hill's top commissions were well-versed in popular taste via pattern books.

A glance at this home's elevations and plans confirms its intent to show off the wealth and taste of its owners. What sets the design intent of this house apart from that of the middle-class row house of the previous example is really a matter of scale. The two floors shown here total over 5,000 square feet, which could nearly double if the basement and attic levels were fully developed to yield maximum usable space.

Although clearly designed for a high-level budget, this plan addresses all of the same basic needs and functions that a typical middle-class Victorian family would require. Although Comstock's book gave no cost estimate for its construction, it is useful to compare it to the largest example from the Newsoms' pattern book (of the first two examples), which was estimated to cost $15,000; by comparison, this one has about twenty percent more space. Although it was considered expensive at the time, it still pales in comparison to some

of the biggest Nob Hill extravaganzas that supposedly cost more than two hundred times that much. As the third example of average sizes and costs, this house is typical for the upper class.

While its style is probably best described as a hybrid, its Eastlake label would be more exact if it included the word Stick, for that influence is predominant on the façade. Flat, linear moldings crisscross much of it, and they are intended to reflect the real structural elements within the walls behind them. Simple flat moldings also outline and extend the window openings, linking those of the tower to its cornice. The decoration of the dormers and gables features arching, fretsawn designs that reflect the Gothic-influenced sensibility of some Stick/Eastlake designs. In fact, the steep pitch of the roofline, and the numerous spiky finials, share that influence. Pierced by gabled dormers, the squared tower's hipped roof recalls the Châteauesque style of the famous old Cliff House that burned in 1907.

The building materials of the house appear to be mostly wood, partially detailed to simulate masonry construction, which was often painted to resemble stone. However, the choice of building materials could vary widely by location. In the eastern states the house would be more likely to be executed in brick and stone. Most of the façade's windows appear to have art-glass panels in the upper sash; near the center, an art-glass roundel window opens into a second-floor room.

On the plan, a vestibule between two front-doorway openings suggests inner and outer sets of front doors (the panelized design of an outer one is visible). Once inside the house, the primary room organization around an oversized entry and stair hall permits an easy circulation flow conducive to entertaining large groups. The decoration of the hall was key to aesthetically blending the adjoining rooms together; most of its impact would be created by architectural details such as wall paneling, possibly carvings, and the design of the main staircase (probably lit by art-glass panels at its landing). There would be several well-chosen pieces, such as a tall gilt pier mirror, a side table or console, and some fancily carved hall chairs. In a house of this stature, upper wall and ceiling areas would be embellished with a showy treatment of rich fabric, wallpaper, stenciling, or handpainting (or perhaps a combination of these). Imposing, gilt-framed artwork and statuary on pedestals would be lined up under the glow of so-called gasoliers. Flooring could feature oriental rugs over inlaid hardwood floors, or might be covered with fitted (wall-to-wall) carpeting edged in matching borders.

Rooms at either side of the front door would be set up to receive visitors in addition to their use by the family. The library was suitable for the reception of male or business callers, while women would be led into the front parlor. The decoration of each area would reflect its gender associations: dark colors, wood paneling, heavily scaled furniture, and perhaps a worldly, exotic theme might be chosen for the decoration of the library. The use of the front parlor by women would guide its decoration toward a more demure floral theme, with softer colors, fabrics, and delicately scaled furniture (with alternative use as a music room).

Opening into this parlor through a wide doorway is a much larger sitting room with a fireplace at the far end, and a large rounded bay window on axis with the adjoining dining room. Because of their close spatial relationship, this large room's decoration would tend to be a compatible variation of the front-parlor scheme. Connecting to both the hall and sitting room, the very large dining room's decoration would most likely expand on the rich colors and wood paneling of the front hall. The plan's formality and the large-scale rooms of this floor suggest that the family would also have an informal family sitting room on the second floor.

The service wing for the live-in domestic staff included a rear staircase, butler's serving pantry, the main kitchen, scullery, and food storage areas. An outside covered porch is alongside the kitchen. Although not shown on the plan, the rear stairway would have extended down to basement and service areas, dedicated to laundry and ironing, coal, and miscellaneous storage needs. In addition to these functions, the basement level may also have contained servants' living quarters.

Separated from these utility areas, the lowest level of this house may have had sufficient remaining space for additional entertainment areas, such as a multi-use ballroom space, perhaps a billiard room, or a children's playroom. These rooms would connect to the main level by another flight below the main staircase.

Upstairs, the plan continues the generous scale of the entry hall, opening into spacious "chambers" (or bedrooms) in each of its corners. It is surprising that such an elegant house had only one bathroom; the dearth of such facilities, while soon to change, was not uncommon at this date even in larger houses.

Possibly used for children's bedrooms, these small rooms at the back may have been assigned to servants. Another location for servants' bedrooms would be on the attic level (not seen on the plans), which appears to suggest a series of rooms. Frequently located in the spacious attic quarters created by lofty Victorian roofs were also children's play and school rooms. For children lucky enough to live in them, the myriad spaces of homes like this were magical worlds for exploration.

did not go unnoticed by the City's builders and real-estate developers, who built many tracts of single-family homes as well as multiple-unit dwellings (typically called flats) as either speculative income property, or sometimes purely as investments for resale.

A leader of many early residential-building campaigns was an organization called The Real Estate Associates (a.k.a. TREA), which began its life as a homestead association in the mid-1860s. However, it became one of the City's largest housing developers. Part of the reason for its strength lay in the business acumen of its founding members, who contributed valuable skills in real estate, accounting, and insurance. This group's shift toward building houses came in the 1870s; it constructed hundreds for a wide range of income brackets.

At that time, TREA's prices for single-family homes ranged from about $3,500 for the least expensive cottage, to almost $10,000 for the largest, usually freestanding mansions or so-called villas. Most, however, were of the more typical row-house style, aimed at middle- to upper-middle-class buyers who could afford the $5,000 to $7,000 price range largely determined by location and lot size. Although some of their housing tracts were in the Western Addition and Pacific Heights areas, the greatest number of TREA homes were built in the vicinity of the Mission District. Variations of the popular Italianate style were used in the majority of their homes. TREA eventually folded in 1881.

Responsible for building over four thousand of San Francisco's Victorian homes mostly in the 1880s and 1890s was Fernando Nelson, who was trained as a carpenter and began building houses while he was still a teenager. In a practice shared by other builders, Nelson devised certain wood details and embellishments that became his signature—carpentry effects that have since helped to identify them. Most of his homes were modest cottages and row houses, and the surviving majority are located in some neighborhoods of the Mission District and adjoining areas of Noe Valley or Eureka Valley (now the Castro District).

An innovation in nineteenth-century home-building techniques, balloon-framing helped hasten the building of Victorian San Francisco. It was so named because of the speed by which it allowed houses to go up ("like a balloon"). Originating in the Midwest, it made shortcuts in wood-frame construction possible. Earlier, the standard way to build a house required the in-ground anchoring of timbers at each corner, then assembly of cross-beams and uprights, all using labor-intensive mortise-and-tenon construction.

Manufacturing innovations of the Industrial Revolution produced machine-made nails and lumber milled to standardized sizes. With a minimum of cross-bracing, builders could quickly assemble wall sections comprised of simply framed vertical studs. When complete, each wall section was easily hoisted into place as a support for the roof structure. Further secured by the application of siding, the walls and roof structure of the house were then more than sufficiently strong to hold it together.

Soon after balloon-framing appeared, a variation called western-platform framing was introduced in house construction in the southern and western United States. It allowed the building to be constructed one story at a time, with each floor becoming a supporting platform for the one above. Homebuilding in the age of the machine was assisted in other ways; mass-produced ornaments of either wood or plaster for both interior and exterior applications became integral to the Victorian-design vocabulary.

SOURCES OF VICTORIAN HOUSE PLANNING AND DESIGN

The power of fashion cannot be overrated, and Victorian San Francisco was as expressive of popular taste as anywhere else in America. Although occasionally a bit behind the cutting edge in its timing, interest in what was fashionable was invariably extended to its architecture. At a time when the western world was at the threshold of a long-term vogue for historic-revival styles, the City entered its first phase of major growth. Like most of America, the City's resulting romance with historic revivalism would persist for the duration of the nineteenth century.

Once ready to build, prospective homeowners who had secured a lot needed to consider issues of design along with possible sources for ideas, advice, and, of course, the necessary building plans. As might be expected, the wealthiest citizens were those most likely to hire an architect to create a custom-built statement to express their wealth and standing in the community. Showy as such results could and would be, they were largely in the minority. However, it is notable that the design sources for ideas expressed in these rarified projects were often the same ones as those affecting the planning and appearance of more modest homes.

Local architects and builders subscribed to important national trade periodicals, such as *Scientific American Architects and Builders Edition,* published between 1885 and 1905. Such publications influenced taste and practice in home design and construction across the country.

On the West Coast, the *California Architect and Building News* was published between 1880 and 1900, with a goal of dispelling "any misconstrued notions which challenged the abilities of the region's profession" and showcased its most innovative new projects. In addition to the building trade, it is notable that there was also a significant audience among prospective homeowners for these publications. By and large, they brought fashionable taste to the emerging streetscapes of San Francisco.

An early media event was triggered in 1880 by the serial publication of *Pelton's Cheap Dwellings* in San Francisco's daily *Evening Bulletin.* This pattern book presented a series of very low-cost house plans by an architect named John Cotter Pelton, Jr., and had an undeniable impact on the local building scene. The book's emphasis was on decidedly modest dwellings, which ranged from a tiny three-room cottage that supposedly could be constructed for $585, to middle-class-size domiciles that were to cost only two or three times that amount. With its construction budgets so much less than those of the competition, *Pelton's Cheap Dwellings* caused a furor among the local architectural establishment, who disputed its claims that decent housing could be built for such low prices. Despite these protests, many houses built to Pelton's designs subsequently appeared in many of San Francisco's working-class neighborhoods.

It was unusual for a pattern book to originate in California at the time. While most architectural libraries within the state contained a wide selection of such books, most were typically published on the East Coast. Another important exception was an influential collection of house plans locally published in 1884 called *Picturesque California Homes.* It was the work of the prolific architects (and brothers) Samuel and Joseph C. Newsom, who had offices in San Francisco and Oakland.

Showing the prevailing eclecticism of that date in terms of architectural style, the Newsoms' book incorporated a mix of Italianate, Eastlake, and Queen Anne characteristics into its various plans. Their designs ranged widely in projected costs from $700 to $15,000, and examples were included that were suitable for narrow city lots as well as sprawling country estates. In general, the work of these brothers comprises some of the most original and creative domestic designs of the period.

Dating to the same year their pattern book was published is their most famous project: the William Carson house in Eureka, California, an extraordinary wooden pile quite suitable for a lumber baron. Today, it is quite possibly the most famous Victorian house in America.

LIVING IN THE VICTORIAN HOUSE

The examples taken from period plan books illustrate three Victorian-era houses that would have been quite typical in San Francisco, and to some extent elsewhere in the Bay Area. The first is a design for a modest three-room cottage in the Stick/Eastlake style. With the exception of its façade, which has the characteristic linear elements of the style, the plan's no-frills sensibility was clearly designed to save space as well as money. It was not uncommon for a family to use the parlor and dining room as bedrooms when needed.

The second plan for a typical middle-class Victorian row house suggests a higher standard of living, for the house had a double parlor and a rear servant's staircase. Also, an entry vestibule appears to have space for both an inner and outer front door. With four separate bedrooms and the potential for more (if the functions of some first-floor rooms were shared), this house is designed to accommodate a fairly large family. The space suggests that a live-in servant could have been included, although day help was more common for the middle class. The two storeys are built over a ground-floor basement that incorporates a laundry room and storage; many such spaces would later be converted to garages.

The third and largest house plan embodies the Victorian ideal of having a separate room for almost every function. Entertaining was important, and the gracious distribution of space centers on a large entry and stair hall, opening on either side to a parlor and other reception rooms, and leading to an oversize dining room. The separate service wing at the rear of the house contains the kitchen area and the back stairway; the pair of rooms next to it on the second floor could be used for either servants or children. The attic and basement levels of this house would have contained utilitarian rooms for the use of servants, but could also have accommodated children's play and/or school rooms.

Although these plans provide good information about the functions and organization of Victorian households, they can only tell a limited story. Other variations abounded, not the least of which were the multiple-unit flats so common in San Francisco. Some of the most expensive flats in the best neighborhoods were far larger than many single-family dwellings, and many also had space for live-in servants. Although flats tended to be rental housing, one of the units was often occupied by the building owner. Of course, grandly scaled flats in multiple-unit buildings became prime targets for subdivision into smaller apartments, a process that has undoubtedly saved many Victorian buildings from destruction. A subdivided old house is certainly better than no old house at all.

Gothic Revival Style
A Fusion of Romanticism and Historicism

Perhaps more than any other Victorian house style, the Gothic Revival is tinged with romantic ideas of the past. Considered by many as an improbable choice for a house, the style became one of the nineteenth century's least understood and most maligned. To understand the forces that brought it into being in America, it is necessary to look back to England and realize that the first phase of the Gothic Revival was already under way there by the middle of the eighteenth century. Because Gothic cathedrals were an ongoing presence not only in England but also in most of Europe, the perception of the style was naturally very different from its reception in America.

The mid-eighteenth century popularity of the so-called Gothick style in England was largely due to its association with romantic literature and to some extent with the fashionable Rococo style. A source of various fanciful design motifs for the decorative arts, Gothick taste contributed a sense of whimsy and romance that was far removed from its origins.

The Gothick taste for the picturesque interested architect and author Batty Langley (1696–1751), who published his ideas in early versions of pattern books after observing and writing about medieval buildings. His books showed how various Gothick forms could be creatively adapted for small buildings or "eyecatchers" intended to be seen at a distance in the parklike landscapes that were an important part of great English estates. Langley influenced other English architects, and some of them developed similar ideas that adapted Gothick forms to small structures. While their books are known to have circulated in colonial America, their impact on popular taste at that time proved minimal; in our early days of settlement (particularly in Virginia), a few modest church buildings were constructed with interpretations of Gothic forms, but little Gothick whimsy.

The Gothic Revival as a housing style became more evident in the later eighteenth century in England through Horace Walpole (1717–1791). Best known as a writer, Walpole also became a tastemaker as a result of his long-term remodeling of his country house in Twickenham, resulting in the extraordinary Gothick icon called Strawberry Hill. This improbable confection of pointed tracery-filled windows and plaster facsimiles of fan-vaulted ceilings was of his own design. Both Walpole and the house, which is now open to the public, gained much celebrity. In 1764, he published his "Gothic" novel *The Castle of Otranto,* in which the atmospheric setting is that of his own home. This genre of dark, mysterious intrigues set in distant times and in shadowy Gothic-style settings became immensely popular; it was copied by many other authors and helped lay the foundation of America's taste for romantic historical styles.

Americans were eager to establish themselves as being civilized. Guiding much of nineteenth-century taste was the prevailing thought that an assimilation of Europe's historic architectural styles might help to hide our lack of a cultural past. This was one reason why many Americans selected foreign styles for their homes.

An important force behind the rise of the Gothic Revival as a domestic style in America was the Scottish novelist and poet Sir Walter Scott (1771–1832), whose works romanticized the medieval period and brought Gothic imagery to life. He became one of America's most widely read authors, and it was through his stories that the Gothic style was transformed beyond its ecclesiastical associations and guided toward its use as a domestic style.

Professional American architects' interest in the Gothic Revival developed slowly. Transplanted Englishman Benjamin Henry Latrobe (1764–1820), best known as an early Greek Revival architect, was the designer of Sedgeley, this country's first Gothic Revival house (now destroyed), which was built in

Fig 1

Fig 2

Fig 3

Fig 4

Fig 5

Fig 6

Fig 7

Fig 8

Fig 9

21. Gothic Revival details (1851). Accompanying the design of a so-called Old English Cottage, these designs appear in the popular pattern book called *The Model Architect* by Samuel Sloan, a Philadelphia architect. Floor plans and exterior views were also included to help prospective homeowners and builders choose and envision the finished house. Although more complete sets of drawings were often available for a fee, only pattern-book drawings were commonly used to guide the actual construction. The largest of these Carpenter Gothic details, an elevation of the entrance porch, shows the characteristic pointed-arch form in the inset panels of a wide front door. Above it, a bargeboard (or vergeboard) decorates the gable's steep pitch. Other Gothic-style details include the oversized, double-ended finial skewered through the gable peak, diamond-paned window sash, and the "drip" molding seen above the double window at the upper right.

22. Elevation drawing of a "Cottage-Villa in the Rural Gothic Style" (1850). This classic Gothic Revival house by architect A.J. Davis appeared as Design XXIV in the important pattern book compiled and written by A.J. Downing called *The Architecture of Country Houses*. Built for Wm. J. Rotch, Esq. of New Bedford, Massachusetts, the house had an estimated cost of $6,000. Downing remarked that the "bold and spirited effect" of the "high-pointed" central gable "would be out of keeping with the cottage-like modesty of the drooping, hipped roof, were it not for the equally bold manner in which the chimney-tops spring upwards." The general composition of this façade was widely copied. Atop the roof, an open area enclosed by a pierced Gothic-style railing "commands a view of the harbor of New Bedford." Opening onto the pair of covered verandas at either side is a drawing room at the left with an equal-size dining room at the right, which flank a central hall; all these rooms interconnect through wide doorway openings fitted with pocket doors.

23. *(Opposite)* Frisbie-Walsh House (The Captain Walsh House), Benicia, California (c.1849). Dating to the time of the Gold Rush and the brink of California's statehood, this Carpenter Gothic gem is the oldest house in Benicia, and it still stands on its original site. Closely related to pattern-book designs favored by A.J. Downing, this façade is the narrow end of a T-shape plan flanked by open verandas. Striking shadows highlight the Gothic tracery of the bargeboard, which frames the front parlor's delicate bay window and the tall, arching window of a front bedroom. Now operated as a bed-and-breakfast inn, this is thought to be one of three virtually identical houses that were prefabricated on the East Coast, shipped in sections, and later assembled in different Bay Area locations. The Vallejo home in Sonoma is the only other survivor, which was built in 1851 for the region's prominent local Californio leader, General Mariano Guadalupe Vallejo. It is open to the public.

24. Detail of paired dormers at the Frisbie-Walsh House. Above one of two covered verandas, this pair of dormers pierces through the roof's overhang to bring light to a second-floor bedroom. A curling line of fretsawn ornament outlines each dormer's small gable peak.

25. Window detail at the Frisbie-Walsh House. A simplified version of a typical Gothic Revival detail, "drip" molding emphasizes a window. Taking its name from both the way it "drips" down the window's sides and sheds dripping water, the molding is terminated by short, horizontal returns.

26. The Webster House, Alameda, California (1854). The oldest surviving house in this East Bay island community, this Gothic Revival cottage was prefabricated on the East Coast and shipped around Cape Horn to be assembled here. A local historical monument, it was first owned by Deacon John Nelson Webster (related to Daniel Webster), who was an early leading citizen of Alameda. Like other cottages of its early date and style, its design was probably adapted from a pattern book. The icicle-like pendant drops of the bargeboards enliven the three gables, and the cut-out shapes of the porch posts and connecting arches dramatize the façade. Operated as a bed-and-breakfast inn and coffee house, the house is set back from the street in a garden shaded by mature trees.

27. The Lathrop House, Redwood City, California (1863). Now in the downtown center of a community south of San Francisco that began as a lumber port about 1850, this house was built in 1863 by Benjamin G. Lathrop, a prominent early citizen who helped establish Redwood City as the first county seat of San Mateo County and was also a founder of the Southern Pacific Railroad. A solidly executed Gothic Revival design, the house boasts many characteristic features: a steeply pitched roof, multiple gables topped with delicately turned finials, "drip" moldings above the windows, and lacy cut-out bargeboards that embellish each gable. Both the front and side porches are handsomely proportioned and incorporate shallow, pierced arches that spring from octagonal porch posts and a low pierced rail that encloses their roofs. The house is open to the public.

28. Detail showing porch post, arches, and upper railing of the Lathrop House. The Gothic quatrefoil (or four-lobed) motif decorates the shallow arches of the porch and is repeated in the railing directly above. Note also the Gothic elegance of the octagonal porch posts with delicate capitals.

29. Mosswood (Moss Cottage), Oakland, California (1863-1864). Possibly the finest example of a Gothic Revival house still standing in California, this splendid building sums up the best of the style inside and out. Mosswood was built as a country estate for J. Mora Moss, a San Francisco businessman who came to California from Philadelphia. Designed in 1864 by architect Stephen H. Williams, it clearly demonstrates his expertise in the Gothic style. Its overall massing indicates that the large projecting bay and roof of the library at the right were skillfully added to the original house, for the façade was originally entirely symmetrical. Mosswood has a modest, cottage-like appearance reinforced by the prominent roof and horizontal-design elements. One of the impressive details is the pierced and snaking bargeboard of the central gable, handsomely integrated with the large finial that emulates the crocket of a Gothic cathedral. A city landmark since 1975, today, this remarkably preserved house has been incorporated into a recreation area of Mosswood Park, where some of the original trees and plantings for the house still survive. The house is not presently open to the public.

31. Detail of three side gables of Mosswood. The delicate open curves of the bargeboard on the gable at the right is a simpler version of the one on the façade. Rising from the side of the library bay at the lower left, the ornate gable at the center repeats all of the decorative elements in the bay.

30. Detail of the library window at Mosswood. Revealing the skill with which the details of this house were conceived and executed, the carving above this window shows how the sinuous movement of the façade's central bargeboard was used on a smaller scale. Accented with art glass that repeats the three-lobe shape of the top transom lights, the narrow windows retain their original folding inside shutters.

32. Front stairs and main entry doors of Mosswood. Reaching out in a wide welcome, this stairway uses characteristic Gothic motifs that are expertly handled to maximize their impact without eclipsing the effect of the overall design. The rhythmic arcading of the railing is repeated and terminated by the square newel posts. On either side of the front doors are massive brackets pierced with oversize quatrefoil cutouts (see fig. 29). Enclosed by a deeply molded surround, the simple, elegantly detailed doors have a large glass transom that provides ample natural light for the front hall. Among the architect's handwritten notes about the house, dated February 1864, are these comments about the exterior, which was "painted white with a tinted trim. White paint set off to advantage the carved brackets, the fretwork, the ornate molding, and the silver-plated hardware."

33. Detail of the parlor ceiling reflected in the mantel mirror at Mosswood. An appreciation of the original elegance of this room can be readily imagined from the sumptuous details that remain. Above a white marble mantel, delicately carved with Gothic motifs, this huge mirror rises to the ceiling. Its crown of gilded plaster foliate scrolls and beading is centered with a woman's head. Reflected in the mirror at the opposite end of the room is an identical crown used as a window cornice set into a shallow bay. Additional opposing windows are also fitted with matching gilded cornices. The ceiling has Gothic-style plaster rib-vaulting, and its intersecting ribs are accented with bosses.

34. Detail of the library ceiling at Mosswood. A remarkable artistic tour de force, the library is the most intact and stunning room in the entire house. The handpainted ceiling panels in the center depict lively cherubic figures involved with various arts and sciences (see fig. 35). These panels suggest the work of a sophisticated designer influenced by England's Aesthetic Movement that was then fashionable. The panels on either side of the center may once have been gilded.

35. Detail of the library-ceiling panels at Mosswood. The fine craftsmanship with which the room's woodwork was executed is especially apparent in this detail. The three handpainted panels seen here represent (from the top) painting, ceramics, and chemistry. The use of images that symbolize the artistic, intellectual, or scientific worlds were considered appropriate decoration for a library.

36. Detail of the library bay window at Mosswood. This view shows the interior of the bay window that was added to the façade (see fig. 29). A frieze of stylized flowers in the manner of Christopher Dresser decorates the upper walls.

37. Detail of the stair railing at Mosswood. At the second floor, a deeply carved, serpentine grapevine decorates the base of the balustrade. The panels at the sides of each stair tread are also intricately carved. Although more detailed, the Gothic arcades of the railing resemble those of the front steps (see fig. 32). Above the stairs, a skylight floods light through the center of the house and down into the first-floor stair hall.

38. The Boyd Gate House, San Rafael, California (1879). As might be suggested by its late date, this house could be considered an evolved version of the mid-nineteenth-century Gothic Revival cottages discussed in this chapter. It certainly shares many of their features, such as windows with pointed arches, "drip" moldings, covered verandas, and a steeply pitched roof with ornamented gables. However, there is also an unmistakable influence of the Stick/Eastlake style in its detailing, seen in the brackets, braces, gable trusses, and veranda railings. Called a gatehouse because of its corner site at the imposing gates to a large estate called Maple Lawn, it may have actually functioned as a guesthouse. Ira B. Cook built this house as an improvement to the estate he had purchased in 1871, which possibly dated to the 1850s. It was after Cook's daughter Louise had inherited the property and married John Franklin Boyd that it became known as the Boyd estate. Further improvements were made to Maple Lawn; its grounds became known as Boyd Gardens and gained a widespread reputation for their fruit trees. In 1905, to honor their sons Seth and John, who had died as teenagers, the Boyds donated this house along with much of their adjoining property to the city of San Rafael as Boyd Memorial Park. Although the Gate House remained intact, the main Boyd house was extensively remodeled by the Boyds' daughter, Louise A. Boyd (a famous Arctic explorer), and was later acquired by the San Rafael Elks Club. Today, the Gate House is the headquarters of the Marin County Historical Society and is used as its museum. A new museum structure is being planned for an adjacent site, which will allow the Boyd Gate House to be restored as a house museum.

39. Detail of the rear and side gables of the Boyd Gate House. Carpenter Gothic seems a particularly apt term here, for almost every possible effect of machine-milled and fretsawn woodworking has been lavished on this house; the fringe ornamenting the veranda's roof is like a wooden version of iron cresting.

40. Gate and fence of the Boyd Gate House. The massive scale of the granite base and wrought-iron construction of this fence at first seems inappropriate for the picturesque and rather modest wooden cottage next to it. Yet considering its original purpose as the gatehouse and this fence at the corner of a large estate, it makes more sense. Gothic elements include the pointed arch formed by the closed gates, the quatrefoil motifs, and the various spiky finials that appear throughout. A photograph of about 1880 shows both the Gate House and this fence in place, so it is likely that the two were planned to go together.

41. The Mark Hopkins mansion, San Francisco (built 1878; destroyed 1906). This wooden palace atop Nob Hill, designed by the firm of Wright and Sanders, was built for Mark Hopkins (one of the Big Four railroad barons) and his wife, Mary, who was known for her extravagant taste. On a heroic scale, it incorporates numerous elements of the Gothic Revival style: a steep, dormered roof, the medieval French forms of its towers and other spires, the arching glass form of the porte cochère and attached conservatory at the left, and much of the window detailing in the upper floors. Its exterior incorporates Gothic detailing with the connecting vertical moldings and robust bracketing of the Stick/Eastlake style combined with Chateauesque massing. The pinnacle of Victorian extravagance in pre-quake San Francisco, the house had few rivals. On the same footprint as its successor, the Mark Hopkins Hotel (1927), it was sited close to the uphill corner for easier front entry because of the hill's steep grade. In this view part of its stone retaining wall is seen along the steep block of Mason Street, between California and Pine (at the right, a portion of the Leland Stanford mansion is visible).

42. Detail of the retaining wall for the Mark Hopkins mansion. Still marked by the slender Gothic tower with its original iron finial, the southeast corner of the Hopkins property (mid-block on Pine between Powell and Mason Streets) gives the impression of an impenetrable fortress. Easily missed by today's passersby on busy one-way Pine Street, this monumental retaining wall (perforated by a few window and door openings along this block) is a last vestige of the Mark Hopkins mansion. At the right was the Leland Stanford mansion, which is today the site of the Stanford Court Hotel. Organized by Stanford, the California Street Cable Railway opened in 1878, linking the financial district with the heights of Nob Hill by cable car, and this line is still running. Utilizing the considerable skills of their own engineers from the Central (later Southern) Pacific Railway, Stanford and Hopkins collaborated on the construction of these massive Sierra granite retaining walls around the lower slopes of their parcels, which remain intact. In fact, the walls are so structurally sound that when the Mark Hopkins Hotel site was first being developed in the 1920s, its builder was unable to remove even part of it by blasting, so it was incorporated into the project. The Mark Hopkins mansion was a residence for only fifteen years; in 1893, the family gave the building as the site for an art school that became the California School of Fine Arts; today it is the San Francisco Art Institute (now on Russian Hill's Chestnut Street).

44

1799 outside of Philadelphia. Ithiel Town (1784–1844) produced an important Gothic design for Trinity Church (1816) on The Green in New Haven, Connecticut, that set a new standard of Gothic authenticity considered appropriate for churches. Between 1829 and 1835, Town was in a partnership with Alexander Jackson Davis (1803–1892). Their firm specialized in public buildings, but in 1832, its first notable residential commission was Glenellen, a Gothic Revival country house (now destroyed) built for Robert Gilmore near Baltimore. A visit by Gilmore to Sir Walter Scott's house Abbotsford had inspired the choice of this style for his home. An influential residential prototype for the next three decades, Glenellen was appropriately sited in a recreation of a picturesque English landscape, complete with a romantically "ruined" Gothic-style gatehouse.

Alexander Jackson Davis became America's leading residential Gothic Revival architect. He designed Lyndhurst in Tarrytown, New York, overlooking the Hudson River, which is today considered America's finest Gothic Revival house. Lyndhurst was built in two phases, and for two different clients. The first, General William Paulding, had Davis design a summer residence that was completed in 1838. Described at that time as a country villa "in the pointed style," the elegant veranda-shaded, gray marble house was widely admired. Davis also designed its Gothic-style furnishings. The second phase of building occurred in 1864, when George Merritt commissioned Davis to enlarge the house. The addition of a large square tower helped retain the integrity and scale of the expanded design. The house (now open to the public) was later owned by Jay Gould. An enthusiast for the Gothic Revival, who admired the works of A.J. Davis, was Andrew Jackson Downing (1815–1852), who became a highly influential tastemaker throughout America. Trained in horticulture, he became a skilled landscape architect for the estates along the Hudson River. He expanded his field to include architecture and published his well-received "pattern book," *Cottage Residences,* in 1842.

His last and most important book was *The Architecture of Country Houses* published in 1850. The house designs covered thirty-four different plans organized into three groups: cottages, farmhouses, and villas. The predominant style of the plans was Gothic Revival, and the association of the cottage styles with rural settings foreshadowed America's tendancy to solve urban problems with suburban solutions.

Late in life, Downing met architect Calvert Vaux (1824–1892) in England. Vaux was well-versed in the vocabulary of medieval buildings as well as of landscaping, and the two shared many ideas. Shortly before Downing's death in a boating accident, they formed a brief architectural partnership. Afterwards, in carrying on Downing's work, Vaux produced his own successful pattern book called *Villas and Cottages* (1857), which was to become quite influential on house design in the Hudson River Valley. Other pattern books followed Downing's success, most notably *The Architect* by William Ranlett (1847), *Rural Architecture* by Lewis F. Allen (1852), *The Model Architect* by Samuel Sloan (1852), and *Rural Homes* by Gervase Wheeler (1853).

Another pivotal figure of the Gothic Revival was Englishman Augustus Welby Northmore Pugin (1812–1852). Highly competent in handling ecclesiastical commissions, Pugin was able to launch his architectural career during a church-building movement in England that promoted the use of the Gothic Revival style. One of his eight major books, *The True Principles of Pointed or Christian Architecture* (1841), stated that Gothic was the most moral of all architectural styles.

By the time of the 1851 Great Exhibition held in London's Crystal Palace, in which Pugin designed a "Medieval Court," many Californians were already familiar with the fashion for the Gothic Revival. In popular books and periodicals, illustrations featuring pointed Gothic arches and window tracery in domestic settings had been routinely appearing for years. These images were subtly encouraging the taste for historic eclecticism that would nurture American appetites for the coming progression of Revival styles.

In terms of surviving examples, the Gothic Revival is one of the scarcest of the Victorian house styles in the San Francisco Bay Area, and what remains can be hard to find. While most California examples still standing were built after 1850, they are remarkably similar to earlier Gothic Revival houses that survive elsewhere.

Italianate Style

American Homes with Renaissance Ideals

The same cult of the picturesque that influenced American taste for the better part of the nineteenth century and established the Gothic Revival was a primary force behind the long popularity of the Italianate style. Once again, English taste was the initial source of this architectural fashion, which was inspired by romanticized farmhouses and rambling villas of the Tuscan countryside. Popular subjects of paintings and book illustrations, such houses were usually depicted as quaint, almost crumbling structures that appeared to be very old. Most had one or more Italian elements: rounded arches, a simple columned portico or colonnaded veranda, or perhaps a distinctive square tower.

As with the Gothic Revival, much of the appealing novelty of picturesque Italian farmhouses and villas was their contrast with the clean, crisp symmetrical designs of Neo-Classicism, which were obviously inspired by more academically correct interpretations of antique forms. At the beginning of the nineteenth century, English architects began to enjoy more artistic freedom through a greater acceptance of imaginative visions of the past; this sense of freedom would resonate strongly in America. Moreover, the increasing public interest in architectural variety seemed to accelerate with each new decade; popular taste and its culture seem to have a way of devouring new ideas.

One of the earliest English examples of a calculatedly romantic building in the Italian countryside vernacular was a country house called Cronkhill, which was built about 1802 near Shrewsbury in Shropshire. A small house, it was destined to have resounding influence. It was designed by a noted architect of the Regency period, John Nash (1752–1835), who was considered a genius of the picturesque. Among his best-known achievements was his extraordinary remodeling of the Royal Pavilion (1815–1823) at Brighton for the Prince Regent (later King George IV). Its expression of luxury was sufficiently inventive and adventuresome to surpass any subsequent heights of nineteenth-century exoticism.

The significance of what Nash accomplished at Cronkhill can be seen in the siting of the house. Placed to be viewed from a distance across a rolling landscape, the intended effect was that of a centuries-old Italian villa in the English countryside. Whether or not it was convincing was of secondary importance. The concept of Cronkhill being a decoration in the landscape was similar to the Gothick follies created by Batty Langley and others. The idea of houses being fanciful stage sets was implicit in much of Victorian domestic architecture. The Victorian period, rife with opportunities for exploitation, justified all kinds of inventive fantasy, and there was no better place than the past to mine new ideas.

Budding English architects who could afford it made a Grand Tour of continental Europe an essential part of their design education. Throughout the nineteenth century, sketchbooks in hand, serious students of architecture and the arts explored and absorbed the cities, museums, monuments, and landscape. Apparently a revelation for many were the evocative buildings of the Italian countryside; Italy (and Greece), long considered the primary font of Western architecture, were the central focus for almost any architectural study.

A continuation of the long European-inspired tradition of borrowing from antiquity, the Italianate style was a distinct contrast to the purity of ancient Greece that had inspired the Greek Revival. Italianate design sources were actually rooted closer to the architecture of Renaissance Italy, which reached its peak in the sixteenth century. While most of the forms associated with Renaissance-era buildings were classically derived, it was how they reinterpreted the scale and use of ancient forms which set that period's architecture apart.

43. Design for an Italianate villa (1878). Published in the fifth edition of a successful pattern book called *Bicknell's Village Builder and Supplement,* this stately home was designed by architect E.E. Myers of Springfield, Illinois. The book's most expensive house, it was built at a cost of $30,000 for Lewis Thomas on his 2,000-acre farm in Montgomery County, Illinois. With its bounty of characteristic details, this house reads like a textbook version of the Italianate style. The square tower and asymmetrical massing are a variation on the so-called villa format. The finial topping the pyramidal hipped roof of the tower extends its height by almost another storey. The floor plan placed primary public and family living spaces and bedrooms in the front part of the house; servants and utilities were in a rear wing. Outdoor living was enhanced by covered verandas on four separate sides. A large dining room formed the spatial link between the two wings and opened onto verandas on opposite sides for both air circulation and outdoor entertaining.

44. The Meek mansion, Hayward, California (1869). A national and state historic landmark, this finely detailed Italianate villa was built for William Meek, a pioneer of the California fruit industry. As its architect is unrecorded, it might have been adapted from a rather grand pattern-book design. Meek personally brought the first grafted fruit trees to the West in a covered wagon over the Oregon Trail. After he moved the nursery business he had started in Oregon to Alameda County, he developed some important new varieties of cherries, including Royal Anne, and Bing (named after his Chinese cook). This house has many Italianate features, including quoins, a single-story angled bay window, an asymmetrical, multi-columned porch or veranda, windows with arched tops and pedimented caps, and an impressive square tower with fashionable bull's-eye or circular windows. Topped with many-bracketed gables that form "open-bed" pediments (the bottom of their triangular shape is left open), a pair of projecting wings sets off the height of the tower, above the portico.

45. Front-porch detail of the Meek mansion. Between the pair of squared columns a wooden pendant of interlocking circles is suspended like a piece of jewelry. The columns' carved capitals have a motif of acanthus leaves that is derived from the Greek Corinthian order, and dentil molding creates a toothy pattern of light and dark.

46. Designs for window caps (1873). Taken from A.J. Bicknell's pattern book, *Detail, Design and Constructive Architecture,* this selection of window cap patterns shows the variety that was possible. All but two (middle and upper left) are typical of the Italianate style.

47. Detail of an Italianate bay window, San Francisco (1880). In the Alamo Square Historic District, this handsome angled bay is a late variation of the Italianate. The pair of round-arch windows are topped with a panel containing a woman's head supported by stylized leaves. This panel, and most of the other ornaments, such as the swags above the side windows, were made of a durable version of cast plaster.

48. The Pardee Home, Oakland, California (1868). This dignified Italianate villa is considered the finest house of its type still standing in Oakland. Enclosing spacious grounds that have survived intact, the front gate and picket fence are exact copies of the originals. Behind the house are a tapering-sided tank house (for water storage) and a carriage house. Masonry-like details include the corner quoins as well as all the wood siding, which has been scored to resemble blocks of stone. In addition, the original stone-gray paint was laced with sand to give a gritty, textured finish. The projecting central section of the façade is crowned by an open-bed pediment that is duplicated by the one on the cupola, from which one can view Oakland and the waterfront. The flaring front steps lead to a well-proportioned portico with a pair of fluted Corinthian columns that support a balcony and balustrade. The house was built for the prominent Pardee family. Both Dr. Enoch Pardee and his son George were eye, ear, and throat specialists, whose political careers included each serving as mayor of Oakland. George Pardee also became governor of California between 1903 and 1907. The house has been open to the public since 1991.

49. Entry and stair hall of the Pardee Home. Mrs. Pardee avidly collected a diverse range of objects from around the world; an important group of local Native American baskets that once lined this hall were donated to The Oakland Museum. Of all the artifacts in the house the most significant and rare is the hexagonal light fixture hanging at the left, made with very large glass photograph plates of Yosemite Valley views that were taken by the renowned early California photographer Carleton E. Watkins, and assembled by his son. This was a gift to Governor George Pardee as a token of Watkins's appreciation for his leadership in arranging for the state government to buy the contents of Watkins's Yosemite Studio in San Francisco, which were to be taken to Sacramento for conservation. Days before the scheduled move, Watkins's entire studio was destroyed in the 1906 earthquake and fire.

50. Billiard room of the Pardee house. Originally planned and used for billiards, this room later became an upstairs sitting room for guests. It also became a library after 1970, when the Pardees' daughter Madeline converted her father's former first-floor study/library into a bedroom and reinstalled its bookcases here. The original billiard table survives with its cue rack on the wall at the left. While the plaster ceiling rosette is an original feature, the figured wallpaper dates from a 1950s redecoration. The flight of stairs seen in the hall leads up to the cupola room.

51. The John Muir House, Martinez, California (1883). The famous botanist, naturalist, and conservationist John Muir (sometimes called the "Father of the National Park System") made his home here from 1890 until his death in 1914. With a hipped roof (not seen in this view) and handsome detailing, its design is distinguished by a square cupola above a symmetrical façade, edged with quoining and with paired and capped second-floor windows over single-storey first-floor angled bays. The front porch is unusually designed as an angled extension of the bays. Around the top of the house, discreetly set between the brackets of the cornice, narrow windows admit light and air to a lofty attic space. The house and grounds are open to the public as the John Muir National Historic Site.

52. Study at the John Muir House. This was Muir's private second-floor study, the inner sanctum where he did much of his important writing. The landscape over the fireplace was painted by his friend, the renowned California artist William Keith. Family photos line the white marble mantel, the style and detailing of which is typical of Italianate houses. The wallpaper frieze and color scheme are later approximations of the original finishes, which were recreated during the room's restoration. With the exception of Muir's own desk and its chair, most of the period furniture in this room is similar to what was originally here.

53. (Opposite) Office/Library at the John Muir House. This room's walls and ceiling retain their original paneling glowing with the contrasting colors of native redwood. Reached through tall pocket doors from a large front parlor, this room once functioned as the office of Muir's father-in-law, Dr. John Stretzel. The adjoining room seen through the door is an enclosed sunporch that could also be entered from a covered side veranda (see fig. 51).

54. The Fallon House, San Jose, California (1855). Significant for its early date and important history, this restrained Italianate design was built by an early prominent citizen of San Jose named Thomas Fallon, who also became one of its earliest mayors. Like some other American settlers of this period, he married into a wealthy Californio family; the father of his wife, Carmel, was one of the most important Mexican landowners in early California. Fallon was the first man to raise the American flag over San Jose during the Mexican-American War. While most of the detailing of this house is quite simple, its composition and scale reflect the sense of formality associated with the Italianate style. Framed by a lush garden setting, this view belies the fact that San Jose's busy downtown district has long since grown up around the house. The Fallon House is open to the public.

55. Double Italianate row house, San Francisco (c.1870s). This pair of mirror-image, flat-fronted houses shows a typical configuration that was favored by builders and developers. The composition gains importance by the grouping of its front doors and entry stairs at the center of the two façades. The façades are emphasized by the quoining, the repeating segmental arches over the bracketed window caps, and the distinctive hanging finials and dentils of the cornice. Located in the Western Addition of the City, this pair of houses was moved here in the early 1970s under the auspices of the San Francisco Redevelopment Agency. Although the relocation of houses for reasons of "progress" has happened throughout the City's history, this part of town has lost far more than its fair share to the wrecking ball.

56. Italianate row house, San Francisco (1877). Located on the western side of the Mission district, this house was developed by The Real Estate Associates, which started as a Homestead Association but evolved as a large-scale developer. Most of their designs were taken from pattern books, but if committed to the purchase in time, willing buyers could pay extra for upgrades of the design selected. The attractiveness of the façade is emphasized by the quoins and by the projecting entry portico. The characteristic form of its columns, with Corinthian capitals and reverse-fluting (on their lower third) is repeated as pilasters on the wall behind them. The interlocking circles of the balcony railing above the entry is an interesting period alternative to the more conventional turned balusters. The restoration of the building to a single-family house prompted the addition of a new pair of outer front doors that shield a second pair behind them inset with glass panels. (A feature of some Victorian houses, it was understood that the occupants were receiving callers when their outer doors were open.) The rather restrained color scheme derived from the period wisely plays down the added garage.

57. Italianate row house, San Francisco (c. 1875). All the hallmarks of a respectable residence in this style are evident here; all that seems missing is a railing around the top of the entry portico, which could be easily replaced. Part of a similar row that was probably the work of a builder or developer, the house has finely crafted details, including fully modeled Corinthian capitals on the bay window's colonnettes that reflect those on the columns and pilasters of the entry portico. The painted panels below the cornice and the painted quoins emphasize the height of the house. The pedimented window cap above the single window shows how Victorian designers used simple moldings to manipulate effectively a building's proportions.

58. *(Opposite)* The Brune-Reutlinger House, San Francisco (1886). Designed by the prolific local architect Henry Geilfuss, this house presents a very proper Italianate face to the world at a date when San Francisco's version of the Stick/Eastlake style was most in fashion, and the Queen Anne style was already emerging. It was commissioned by a German immigrant named Henry Brune, who had arrived here about twenty years earlier and had become very successful in the wholesale liquor distributing business. It was subsequently sold to William Gallagher, a prosperous Irishman, whose family members remained in the house until 1952. After a dozen years as a Baptist Church, and then narrowly escaping destruction, it was rescued in 1965 by its current devoted owner, Richard Reutlinger, who has made its maintenance and restoration an ongoing priority. National recognition of the work done here has made the house an icon of the Victorian Revival. The fluted columns of its portico have capitals of cast iron; their design is a Classical "hybrid" that is repeated on the capitals of the bay's fluted colonnettes. A set-back from the street allowed the addition of a garage without altering the basement level ballroom; this change redirected the front steps to one side, and expanded the entry level into a more usable raised terrace.

59. *(Above)* The Camron-Stanford House, Oakland, California (1875–1876). This elegant Italianate house remains a representative of the numerous mansions once strung along the curving shore of Lake Merritt. It was originally built for Will and Alice Camron, who subsequently rented the house between 1878 and 1881 to David Hewes, a grading and paving contractor in San Francisco, who used the house for many social functions. Later on the house was purchased by Josiah Stanford (the brother of San Francisco railroad baron Leland Stanford), who would live there for twenty-one years. In 1906 the city of Oakland bought the Camron-Stanford house for the newly organized Oakland Public Museum, which opened in 1910 under the curatorial leadership of Charles P. Whitcomb. A transplanted New Englander, Whitcomb developed a powerful and effective group of period room settings that was widely copied. His interpretation of a Colonial-era kitchen or keeping room in this building was especially popular and influential; his curatorial work here and at San Francisco's De Young Museum is noted for its importance in promoting public interest in the Colonial Revival. The house was vacated when the new Oakland Museum of California was built nearby in 1967; it was restored and reopened to the public in 1978 as a house museum to illustrate life in nineteenth-century Oakland. A superbly detailed example of the Italianate style, this house is asymmetrical in its overall composition. At the right side is a glassed-in conservatory that continues around the side of the house and also connects with the front parlor.

Among its leading practitioners was Andrea Palladio (1508–1580), considered one of the first great professional architects, whose widely published works would have an ongoing influence on English and American architects for more than two centuries after his death. Strongly inspired by Palladio, the Italianate work (mostly on grand public buildings) of English architect Sir Charles Barry represents some of the best early examples of the style from the 1830s and '40s that were widely published and internationally copied. Therefore, if the Italianate style really wasn't new, then the more democratic turn it took in nineteenth-century America was for a greater diversity of building types that extended beyond public buildings and mansions to embrace the urban row house.

Essentially using familiar Classical forms, the Italianate style is relatively easy to recognize. However, it can occasionally be a challenge to distinguish it from other styles that incorporate some of the same elements, such as will be found in the Colonial Revival/Classical Revival and Edwardian Era chapters of this book. It will become apparent that the Italianate is characterized by a more inventive and less academic use of classical forms.

A key element in identifying Italianate houses is to observe the overall form of the windows, which tend to have rather vertical proportions. The most common window shape was with a shallow or "segmental" arched top, but variations included flattened tops with slightly rounded corners, or fully rounded arched tops. Flat-topped windows were also used. Some house designs employ a variety of window shapes. Windows were often used in pairs to provide more light and visual interest.

To emphasize them further, several devices were used. One of the most popular was the use of window hoods, the form of which was quite similar to the Gothic Revival "drip" moldings. The simplest type of window hood employed a wide, flat molding that relied on its own cut-out shape for interest. The most elaborate examples used deeply grooved moldings of a scale similar to those of interior doorway surrounds. Most window hoods had a raised central finial or "keystone" element, much like those seen on the tops of mirrors, chairs, and headboards of Renaissance Revival furniture. Most in fashion at the time, the interior design and furnishing styles of Italianate houses were most likely to be decorated in variations of either the Renaissance or Rococo Revival styles, sometimes both. It should be noted here that the term *Italianate* is used only for the architectural style.

Supported by a pair of small brackets, projecting shelf-like caps were also used to trim out the tops of Italianate windows. This detail was derived from Italian Renaissance architecture. The simplest type of caps were flat-topped, but many variations were used, and those with triangular pediments or arched tops were frequently seen. To save money on urban row houses and elsewhere, capped windows would appear only on the front façade, or wherever they would be most visible from the street. To cast shadows and add visual weight, the windows were constructed to project forward, and most were set off against a rather plain background of clapboard siding or stuccoed brick; some had small brackets under their sills.

More elaborate Italianate windows were framed by heavy casings that completely surrounded them on three sides down to the sill line. Such frames often had complex shapes and detailing at their tops, and many were anchored by flaring details just above the sill. Italianate window frames often included style details of Renaissance Revival furniture, such as supplemental carved ornament.

One of the most characteristic elements of the Italianate style are bay windows with angled sides. The bays could have one or a pair of front-facing windows between the angled windows. More refined examples might include slender columns called colonnettes that were often placed between each window of the bay. Instead of being free-standing, colonnettes were engaged (or attached along their length) to the wood molding behind them. Because most Italianate houses were two-storied, their bay windows would usually extend full height, but examples of single-storey bays on two-storey houses are also seen.

The Italianate entry porch or portico was typically single-storey high, the top of which formed a balcony enclosed by a railing or balustrade. Being the place of entry, front porches were the focal point of the façade. On larger houses, separate porches or verandas might appear elsewhere on the building.

Topped with a version of a capital, some column assemblies were by necessity created on site by carpenters, using only built-up assemblies of moldings. However, the most elegant Italianate designs used adaptations of the Classical Orders for their capitals. While most of these were created from carved or turned wood, others were made of cast iron, which was almost indistinguishable from carved wood when it was painted. Use of cast iron was far more common on mid-nineteenth-century commercial buildings than it was on houses, notably as a primary fireproof structural building material. Modular cast-iron components for entire façades are still seen in some cities' old warehouse districts, most notably in New York's Soho district.

Another characteristic Italianate architectural detail is the use of quoins to accent the corners of a house, thus giving more weight to the overall design. Quoins (derived from the French *coin* or "corner") were decorative devices seen in Italian Renaissance buildings that were shaped and placed to resemble building blocks of stacked stone. The 1863 Morse-Libby house, or Victoria Mansion, in Portland, Maine, and open to the public, is a famous example of an Italianate residence made of stone. Italianate row houses using similar masonry construction, are nicknamed "brownstones" are found mostly in East Coast cities, especially in New York.

60. Detail of the main staircase of the Camron-Stanford House. It was usual for a staircase of this period to be terminated by a newel-mounted light such as the one seen here. The substantial design of the newel post and turned spindles is typical for a grand house, as are the foliate carvings that decorate the side of each stair tread. Note the delicate stenciled fringe on the far wall and the elaborate Renaissance Revival cabinet.

61. Front parlor of the Camron-Stanford House. This is the formal room where visitors would be received. The woodwork throughout this floor has painted graining to represent walnut, with contrasting burled walnut used for the inset door panels as seen on the library door directly ahead. The Anglo-Japanese pattern of the wallpaper frieze (first reproduced for this room) is by the progressive English designer Dr. Christopher Dresser. Inspired by his mid-1870s visit to Japan, the pattern also reflects the influential cross-cultural taste of England's Aesthetic Movement then underway; the peacock feathers also reflect this taste. The plaster ceiling rosette has been effectively polychromed to highlight its design. The unusual chandelier incorporates both oil and gas lights. The richly carved white marble mantel is of the period but is not original to the house. Above it hangs a portrait of Josiah Stanford.

59

62. The main or family parlor of the Camron-Stanford House. At the center of a sequence of three parlors, this is the one that would have been most used by the family, for it is the most spacious room. Dating to the 1970s restoration, the wallpaper frieze and matching "fill" paper below it were reproduced from the 1870s originals that are still intact at Château sur Mer, an important Victorian mansion open to the public in Newport, Rhode Island. The plaster cornice and stenciled decoration on the ceiling were painted to coordinate with the papers. Above the carved white marble fireplace is a gilded Renaissance Revival mirror that is original to the house, and the marquetry cabinet under the painting at the right is also a Renaissance Revival piece. The two slant-back "Turkish" chairs at the left and right are rare for still having their original upholstery.

63. *(Opposite)* The "Hewes Art Gallery" at the Camron-Stanford House. The last of the connected parlors, this room is called the Hewes Art Gallery in honor of the early residents Mr. and Mrs. David Hewes, whose "D. Hewes Art Collection" was the source of inspiration for the things assembled here. Both the paintings and sculptures on display represent the fashionable taste of wealthy Americans who could afford to make a Grand Tour of Europe. They often collected expensive copies of Old Master paintings and Greco-Roman sculpture. They also collected furniture, porcelain, tapestries, and carpets for their homes. The lush red of the walls, the ornate frieze and the gold of the carpet and draperies provide a luxurious background for the paintings and sculpture. Two novel, very American chairs, fashioned from steer horns, lend an unexpected decorative accent.

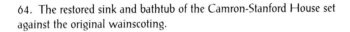

64. The restored sink and bathtub of the Camron-Stanford House set against the original wainscoting.

Large arched or curving brackets sometimes used in pairs and placed under the eaves are a key element of the high cornices that crown Italianate roof lines. Many brackets and other ornaments had decorative curving incised lines made by machine. On modest houses, brackets often replaced columns altogether, and were the support for an overhang above the front door. This detail inspired the term *Bracketed* as a name with which to describe some variations of Italianate style. It is interesting to note that famed American novelist Edith Wharton used "Hudson River Bracketed" (1929) as the title of one of her stories.

Adapted from its use in the Italian countryside, another component of the Italianate style is the *campanile*, or square tower. It was used as an important element of Queen Victoria's famous country house on the Isle of Wight called Osborne House (built 1844–1849). Designed by Thomas Cubitt in collaboration with Prince Albert, who aspired to being an architect, the rambling, stucco-faced Italianate design featured two tall slightly different square towers.

Osborne House became very influential in the British Empire and in America, and the fashion for square towers lasted for over two decades.

Because towers were used on large houses, such houses were often called villas. The term *villa* was in popular use by mid-century, and A.J. Downing attempted to define its American meaning in a chapter of his influential book, *The Architecture of Country Houses* (1850), in which the examples used were Italianate style with square towers.

Square towers were also sometimes incorporated into large Second Empire and Stick/Eastlake style designs across the country. Today, the term *villa* is generally limited to these styles and to large houses that include a prominent square tower in their composition.

A smaller version of a square tower, usually called a cupola, sometimes is used on villas. Like the "lanterns" of earlier periods, the windows of cupolas allow light to flood down into the house.

65. Detail of the dining-room chandelier of the Camron-Stanford House. Showing how the Victorian love of ornament and technical ingenuity could be combined, this fixture was intended for use over a table, so it became a chandelier as well as a reading or task light. It is over seven feet high and uses both oil and gas.

Second Empire Style
The French Connection

Although it was the height of fashion in the Bay Area during most of the 1870s, the Second Empire style was not nearly as well represented in other areas of the Far West as it was in the East and Midwest. The style enjoyed a great vogue in San Francisco, but the 1906 earthquake and fire destroyed the bulk of its most significant examples; others later fell victim to changing tastes and the usual forces of destruction that seem to overwhelm old buildings. The houses illustrated are among the few rare examples that still survive in the vicinity.

The name of the style derives from the period in France known as the Second Empire (1852–1870), the years of the reign of Emperor Napoleon III and Empress Eugénie. All eyes of the fashionable world turned to France in matters of taste, refinement, and dress, and its lasting influence here is still seen in Second Empire-inspired examples of architecture and furnishings. Not only was it the only French style that was adopted by nineteenth-century Americans, it was also one of the few styles that didn't first occur in England.

What chiefly distinguishes the Second Empire style from the otherwise closely related Italianate style is the mansard roof. Mansard roofs generally rise at a very steep angle, usually a full storey in height, before ending in a shallowly hipped or flattened form. Cast-iron cresting was a popular way to trim out the tops. The sides of mansard roofs are either pitched at a straight angle, or are fashioned in a curved—concave, convex, or compound "ogee," or "S"—shape. Their high sides are almost always penetrated by a series of dormers that can have varying shapes.

The high visibility of the roofing material on the steep sides encouraged a fashion for repeating shingle patterns. On houses with wooden shingles (most typical in the West) these patterns were often highlighted with paint colors; on masonry houses colored slate shingles were used.

Most mansard roofs conceal a very spacious attic storey that typically contains almost a full floor of space. Commonly used for additional bedrooms as well as for storage, this top floor often included servants' rooms. Separate from issues of style and fashion, the intrinsic appeal of the mansard roof was the way it provided a significant amount of additional space without creating that impression from the street.

The term *mansard* derives from the name of a famous seventeenth-century French architect named François Mansart (1598–1666). By adapting Renaissance forms, he helped transform French architecture from Gothic-based traditions toward a new national style, and he had a far-reaching influence on other architects. Perhaps his most important and fully-realized project on a grand scale was Maison Lafitte, a country house outside Paris (built 1642–1646), where the mansard roof is fully developed.

Largely because of their novelty and wide publication here, examples of fashionable French architecture and interiors of the Second Empire period had a significant impact on American taste, especially for the well-to-do. As a status symbol, its appeal helped create in America a strong market for collecting French antiques, and a brisk market for good reproductions also developed.

Wealthy Americans visiting Europe quickly became used to the extravagant interiors typical of most fine hotels, which often had a strong influence on their taste in architecture and interior design after returning to America. Most public spaces and suites of rooms in these hotels featured nineteenth-century adaptations or reproductions of lavish eighteenth-centu-

66. Design for a Second Empire-style house (1878). Published in *Bicknell's Village Builder and Supplement*, this house was designed by architect D.B. Provoost of Elizabeth, New Jersey, and is typical of many examples aimed at the middle-class market. Above a bracketed cornice a concave-sided mansard roof is highlighted with bands of patterned shingles in various colors, and there is a top cresting of interlocking circles. There are two alternative front door styles indicated. The smooth walls suggest the typical finish of painted stucco over brick walls that was common in the East. Connected by a long stair hall, the first-floor plan had a parlor, dining room, and kitchen. On the second floor were two large bedrooms and one small rear bedroom next to a full bathroom. On the partial third floor, there were two small bedrooms across the front and a larger one behind.

67. Second Empire-style row house, San Francisco (1870). With an unusually rakishly concave curve in its mansard roof, this house is a standout. Each side of its two-storey bay is topped by an arching dormer window, and each of the dormers is set into a deeply hooded recess similar to a lady's bonnet of the period. Clever detailing integrates them well into the adjoining cornice, especially the continuation of the dentil molding above each arch. Alternate bands of original patterned shingles, now all painted alike, still remain visible on the sides of its roof. Now located in Pacific Heights, the house was first constructed for Richard Dallams on the lower slope of Nob Hill at the corner of Sutter and Mason Streets near Union Square. As the neighborhood became more commercial and density grew, the house was converted to office space for a doctor and dentist until 1900, when pending redevelopment of its site made either displacement or destruction necessary. Dr. Emma Sutro Merritt moved it here to be her home. One of the first women to practice medicine at the time, she was also the daughter of former mayor Adolph Sutro. In the same way many good old houses could be moved and relocated for less cost than building a new house of comparable quality. Despite the obstacle of the hills, moving houses was more common in San Francisco than in most other cities.

68. Second Empire-style row house, San Francisco (1885). Built by developer Charles Hinkel for George Casser (reputedly for $17,000), this dignified, stunning house is even larger than it appears. Hinkel was one of five brothers who were all owner-builders, and among the most prolific in San Francisco. The sides of the mansard roof on this house have straight rather than curved sides, and in the front, pedimented dormers extend from the cornice to above the roof. The handsome blue and aubergine palette is vividly enlivened by the red-orange shingle patterns on the mansard roof and the flared "French cap" of the first-floor bay window. The impressive side elevation at the right, which includes another bay window, is ornamented to match the façade. The left and right corners of the house are emphasized by vertical panels. Sited on the cusp of the Western Addition and Haight Ashbury districts, this building is in a neighborhood that has many well-preserved Victorian homes. It is San Francisco Landmark Number 190.

69. Design for a Second Empire-style cottage (1878). Designed by architect Lyman Underwood of Boston, this house was published in *Bicknell's Village Builder and Supplement* as a "design for a French cottage," and described as being "simply and conveniently arranged for a small family." It demonstrates how a mansard roof could be successfully applied to a modestly scaled house. Estimated to cost $3,800 (under "ordinary circumstances"), it was specified to be built of wood and to be painted "to harmonize with its surroundings" in a country setting. Like most mansard-roofed houses, this one was designed with a surprising amount of space. Its double entry doors lead through a small vestibule to a square central stair hall. There is a front parlor, a sitting room, and a kitchen adjoined by a long separate pantry. There was also a vestibule leading to the back door. The attic storey behind the mansard roof contained three good-size bedrooms (each with ample closets), a small extra room, and a bathroom.

70. Second Empire-style house, San Francisco (c.1872–1892). This house in the Pacific Heights area is a charming, unusual example of a modest mansard-roofed house that would have been described at the time as a "cottage." Set behind a small iron fence, it recalls the scale of many cottages that once dotted the open hillsides of early San Francisco. The gentle sweep of its mansard roof is echoed in a large, central gable, the many-sided gambrel shape of which gives the façade its most distinctive feature. According to what was published in 1892 by *The California Architect and Building News*, this house was the work of Mooser and Cuthbertson and cost $2,200. Yet, instead of being a brand-new house, the house was instead a rather skillful assemblage of disparate "house parts" salvaged from earlier buildings and grafted onto an earlier house. The house parts had become available as a result of various alterations, demolitions, or relocations that were common around San Francisco throughout the nineteenth century. Today, it remains unclear exactly what existed on the site before this appealing configuration was so cleverly collaged together.

71. The Feusier (or Kenny) Octagon House, San Francisco (c.1850s). A unique survivor for its location, form, and date, this octagonal house enjoys a serene garden setting. On a block of nineteenth-century homes near the crest of Russian Hill, it escaped the destruction of the 1906 earthquake and fire that claimed almost everything around it. As San Francisco Landmark Number 36, this is the oldest of only two remaining octagon houses in the City. America's brief interest in them was largely the result of promotion by the Fishkill, New York, lecturer and writer Orson S. Fowler in his 1848 pattern book *A Home for All, or a New, Cheap, Convenient and Superior Mode of Building*. Similar plans appeared later in at least seven other pattern books. However, only a few thousand octagons were built throughout the country, mostly in the East and Midwest. Fowler extolled the octagon design for its economy, good design, and aesthetics. Originally built by George L. Kenny, it was purchased by Louis Feusier in 1870, and it is his name that is most associated with the house. In the 1880s, Feusier chose the Second Empire style when he enlarged the house, adding another full floor with the concave, fishscale-shingled Second Empire mansard roof on the original two-storey building. The cupola is also octagonal. Today, the stuccoed walls of the lower floors and modified porch and window elements reflect later alterations, but its appeal remains.

(Overleaf) 72. The Lyford House, Tiburon, California (1874). Possessing a complex past with a happy ending, this enchanting house was floated on a barge to its present site in 1957 to avoid certain destruction by a new development in the vicinity of Strawberry Point on Richardson Bay (part of San Francisco Bay) in Marin County just north of San Francisco. Although its scale is small the form of this mansard-roof house and tower suggests that of a Second Empire villa. Note the elaborate finials gracing the dormers on the tower and the dormers at the right. It was first built on part of the 9,000-acre Rancho Corte Madera del Presidio, an 1834 land grant made to naturalized Mexican citizen John Thomas Reed by Governor Figueroa. As the first non-native, non-Hispanic person to settle in the Marin area, Reed's land holdings encompassed all of present-day Mill Valley, Tiburon, Corte Madera, San Rafael, and San Quentin. He married Ylaria Sánchez, daughter of a local official, at Mission Dolores in 1836. One of their children, Hilarita, and her husband, Dr. Benjamin Lyford, were the original builders of this house. After having served as an assistant surgeon in the Civil War, Lyford came to the Bay Area in 1866 to seek his fortune, and he found it by his marriage to the heiress of the largest land holdings in Marin. After their deaths, the house was occupied in the early 1900s by Mrs. Lyford's nephew John Paul and his sister Clothilde, whose live-in servant, Rose Rodríguez, loved John Paul. Upon his death in 1919, Rose inherited eleven acres in Tiburon, where she had been living in a shack. Rose lived long enough to see John Paul's house floated to its new site on her land, which she had arranged to donate as part of a wildlife sanctuary in the vicinity. It is now part of Tiburon's Richardson Bay Audubon Center and Sanctuary, and the Lyford House is open to the public.

73. The Sherman House, San Francisco (1876). This grand house was built for Leander S. Sherman, a prominent early patron of both the San Francisco symphony and opera, who was also the founder of Sherman Clay and Company, one of the nation's oldest and largest music stores. Sited between the Pacific Heights and Cow Hollow neighborhoods, this house is elegantly detailed both inside and out. The pedimented caps of the dormers are supported by delicate turned colonnettes. In 1972, this house was designated San Francisco Landmark Number 49; in more recent years it has been operated as a small hotel.

ry-style rooms and their furnishings, most typically in imitation of the Rococo and French Neoclassical styles. Most middle-class Americans had to be content with our own adaptations of the Rococo and Renaissance Revivals, which were the most fashionable furnishing choices for Second Empire and Italianate houses.

America's love affair with the Second Empire style was intense but rather brief. Because of the architectural prominence of the mansard roof, the big impression it made led to its popularity in American cities and the countryside. Following the Civil War, the style became especially popular for public buildings in the years of the Grant administration (1869–1877), during which time it became known as the "General Grant style." A series of nationwide financial troubles beginning in the early 1870s (particularly the so-called Panic of 1873) helped to cool the public's ardor for the Second Empire style.

74. Music room of the Sherman house. Containing a ballroom-size area of unusual height designed to enhance its acoustics, this stunning addition transformed the Sherman house into a center for San Francisco's social, cultural, and musical life. The room is entered by the pair of staircases at the right from the main part of the house. The crystal chandeliers and ornate wall sconces help establish this magnificent room to a mood of grandeur rarely found in a private house. Shallow plaster beams, aligned with the pilasters below, arch into the cove and cross the ceiling in two directions, forming a series of large coffers. An enormous skylight in the central coffer washes the room in natural light. This room witnessed live performances by some of the greatest musical artists of the day, including Madame Schumann-Heink, Ignace Paderewski, and San Francisco's own Lotta Crabtree, a much-beloved entertainer of the post-Gold Rush years.

76. Design for a Stick-style cottage (1883). This unassuming but rather stylish Stick-style design appeared in a pattern book called *Cottage Houses for Village and Country Homes* by architect S. B. Reed. Its proposed building cost was $750. A characteristic "stick-work" gable truss or brace is mounted on the projecting eaves of a large, forward-facing gable to provide support and strength and also to cast shadows and add to the depth of the design. Vertical board-and-batten siding behind it is cut into points where the boards overlay the horizontal clapboard siding below. It is the structural purpose of these various elements that is the primary decoration of this house. Eastlake-style detailing is seen in the chamfered or beveled edges of all the porch posts, the brackets or braces, and the gable truss.

77. Detail of Stick-style braces, San Francisco. Recently adapted from a period pattern-book drawing, these braces supplement a slender corner-support post of a covered rear porch. Like the braces illustrated in figure 76, these have a simplicity, and sunshine glistens on their chamfered edges. The porch ceiling is fitted with narrow tongue-in-groove boards that interlock for a tight fit.

78. The James Shinn House, Fremont, California (1876). The deep overhanging eaves of this sturdy farmhouse were probably used to fend off the summer sun rather than to make a style statement. Its most compelling feature, the bold central gable overhangs an arch-topped attic window. On the second floor below, a French door leads to a balcony on top of the front porch that is visually extended by a rambling, open-beamed pergola covered with flowering vines, thus wrapping the house with extra shade and fragrance. Built of redwood for James Shinn, the house was once the centerpiece of a 300-acre ranch in the Niles District of Washington Township, now in Fremont. Shinn came to this area in 1856 and established one of the first nurseries in California. Now surrounded by an arboretum that includes a Japanese garden along with some original trees and plantings, the Shinn House is open to the public.

79. Design for an Eastlake row house (1881). This design by local architect John C. Pelton, Jr. is reproduced from a pattern book called *Cheap Dwellings.* Pelton's designs were accepted by the Real Estate Association of San Francisco, which financed and developed thousands of middle-class homes. There was soon a widespread assimilation of Eastlake ideas by many architects, builders, and developers in the Bay Area. This example has in its overall Stick-style form simple, flat-board trim that outlines the façade's structural elements. Most prominent is the front-gable truss fitted with cut-out panels against vertical boards.

80. Detail of a gable on the Nightingale House, San Francisco (1882). Peaked gables like this were used for artful carpentry during the Eastlake-mad 1880s in San Francisco. Their effect could be strikingly similar to the lace and crochet work that were then popular as home crafts. Designed by architect John Marquis, the house was built for developer John Nightingale as his own residence. Standing on a corner in the neighborhood called Mint Hill on the southern edge of the Western Addition, the Nightingale House is San Francisco Landmark Number 47.

81. *(Opposite)* The Westerfeld House, San Francisco (1889). This house is a world-famous icon among San Francisco's Victorian houses. Situated across from Alamo Square in the Western Addition, it was designed in 1887 by local architect Henry Geilfuss for a baker and confectioner named William Westerfeld. The house was recently painted to fulfill the owner's vision of brooding grandeur accented with gold leaf. The structural elements of this house are given vertical emphasis by Stick-style detailing, and beneath a high, panelized cornice containing third-floor windows, a band of vertical siding terminates in an Eastlake-style saw-tooth pattern. The Italianate details include the front portico and columns, the balcony railing with balusters and finials, the pedimented window caps, and the hooded, round-arched window. Above a full-raised basement level are three full floors of living space. The tower has a large room with a high pyramidal ceiling that has a great view of the City. The Westerfeld house is San Francisco Landmark Number 135.

82. Stick-style row house, San Francisco (c.1888). An Eastlake sensibility pervades almost all of the detailing on this Mission District house. The Classical forms that are often adapted in other San Francisco Stick designs are stylized almost beyond recognition here; at the time it was built such abstraction of familiar forms would have made this house seem particularly modern. It was built by a developer named John Coop, who was also the head of the San Francisco Planing Mill. Producers of moldings and other wooden ornament, the company's handiwork enlivens this façade. In typical Stick fashion, the cornice brackets are connected to the windows and other vertical moldings beneath them. The use of simple diagonal lines in the wood panels under the windows is an Eastlake-style detail that also appears on some of the furniture of that style. The rounded forms of the sunburst rays in the gable-like pediment on the entry's shed roof help reflect light off the gold leaf. In the purely decorative gable above the squared bay the inky blue shingled panel disappears into the shadows.

83. Stick-style row house, San Francisco (1897). Part of a row of five buildings built by developer Fernando Nelson in Eureka Valley (called the Castro District), this house contains many of his signature elements. To save money and have them ready for use, Nelson usually had the details made up in large quantities. The details had special names: for example, on the entry portico, the cut-out circles were called "donuts," and the panel above it with rounded ends and circles was called a "button board." What he called "drips" appear between the bay's windows and above the columns of the portico. Also seen here is a semicircular panel outlined by dentil molding that Nelson also favored for his "false gables."

84. Stick-style row house, San Francisco (c.1895). Another characteristic design produced by developer Fernando Nelson, this attractive house is a further example of his widespread use of signature details that were produced in quantity for many of his houses, such as the "donuts," "button boards," and "drips." On the whole, the house shares many elements with figure 83.

85. The Cohen-Bray House, Oakland, California (1884). One of the finest examples of a Stick-style villa remaining in the Bay Area, the house was built as a wedding present for Alfred H. Cohen and Emma Bray by the bride's parents, whose large estate was across the street, and it was continuously occupied by family members. Alfred and Emma's last surviving child, Emelita, lived here until her death in the early 1990s. The predominantly Stick-style design of the house is seen in the simple vertical moldings linking the windows with the brackets of the upper façade, as well as the large peaked gable-brace and the brackets beneath the tower's flared eaves. Eastlake influence is evident in the simple, sawcut detailing of the upper porch posts and small balcony railings of the third floor. The original interior decorative schemes, furnishings, decorative objects, memorabilia, and other archival materials are very significant. A resource for the study of nineteenth-century Bay Area domestic life and taste, the Cohen-Bray house is now the headquarters of the Victorian Preservation Center of Oakland and open to the public.

86. (Opposite) Entry hall of the Cohen-Bray House. The walls and ceiling of the entry hall are richly paneled with redwood that was specifically milled for this room. Unlike most redwood, the curly grain was considered so special that it was presented to Alfred and Emma Cohen as a wedding gift. An Eastlake-inspired arrangement of flat moldings with chamfered edges creates a framework of recessed panels. The tall-case mahogany clock is a family piece. The fashionable Aesthetic Movement motifs of stylized sunflowers are repeated on the woodwork of the adjoining rooms. Also in the Aesthetic taste are the art-glass window with a peacock, a small Eastlake-style ebonized screen concealing a gas heater, and carved and inlaid Chinese furniture. Next to the arched mirror enclosed in the paneled wall the graceful main stairway rises in an alcove; the jog in the wall next to it encloses the back of the dining-room sideboard (fig. 94).

87. Woodwork detail in the entry hall of the Cohen-Bray House. In this view both the beauty of the redwood and the expert carpentry are particularly evident. The built-in arched mirror matches the one illustrated in figure 86, and at the right is a storage cupboard recessed in the wall.

88. Detail of a front-parlor pocket door at the Cohen-Bray House. The woodwork of the front parlor retains its original pale greenish-gray painted finish. The arched sliding pocket doors have an artful arrangement of irregular panels framed by chamfered moldings, and Aesthetic motifs of fans and sunflowers are incised in some of the panels and highlighted in gold leaf. The Aesthetic taste is emphasized by the Chinese table and embroidered folding screen.

89. Detail of the front-parlor ceiling at the Cohen-Bray House. The high quality of carving and inlay in the pediment of the exceptional Pottier and Stymus mirror is apparent here. Sprays of blue flowers accent the ceiling. Looking as if they were handpainted, the sprays were actually cut out of a separate wallpaper pattern and then decoupaged onto the ceiling.

90. Front parlor of the Cohen-Bray House. This room's feeling of lightness, refinement, and pleasing proportions employ an elegant restraint in color and pattern. At the right, the room-wide angled bay window adds much more space than the usual angled or square bays of Italianate and Stick houses, and this type of bay window was to become a standard feature of Queen Anne-style houses. A geometric wallpaper pattern utilizes the coved ceiling to exaggerate the room's height and draw the eye upward. The seating pieces (some of which retain their original upholstery) were supplied by Pottier and Stymus, a prominent New York furniture manufacturer; they also made the very large mirror, although it is not original to this house. After Fernside, the nearby Alameda estate of Alfred Cohen's parents, was destroyed by a fire in the late 1890s, some of its luxurious furnishings were salvaged and brought here.

91. Library at the Cohen-Bray House. This room's rich color scheme features deep red, terra-cotta, and olive greens that harmonize with its dark woodwork. Scenes from famous stories by Sir Walter Scott are depicted on six transfer-printed Minton tiles of the fireplace surround. Built-in walnut bookcases with glass doors contain the library's original book collection. Pocket doors located opposite the bay window wall at the right connect to the central hall and dining room. The way in which this house allows its spaces to be combined for large-scale entertaining is similar to Queen Anne-style house plans.

92. *(Above)* Detail of the library ceiling at the Cohen-Bray House. A wide frieze design with a bronze, olive, gold, and terra-cotta color scheme arches into the ceiling, where it joins another bright floral band. Its leafy background is a foil for a stylized architectural design. Above the gilded picture rail, a painted accent band of terra-cotta underscores the frieze.

93. *(Above, right)* Detail of the central hallway at the Cohen-Bray House. These handsomely paneled doors epitomize Aesthetic and Eastlake design. The swinging doors at the left lead to the back hall and rear service areas. The pocket doors at the right open to the library. In accordance with Aesthetic taste, the "colors of nature" appear in the stylish original wallpaper.

94. *(Below, left)* Dining-room sideboard of the Cohen-Bray House. Made from beautifully grained walnut, this built-in sideboard is the most imposing feature of the dining room. Its recessed placement caused a jog in the wall of the entry hall (see fig. 86). Topped by a reddish marble serving surface, the projecting cabinet with drawers and enclosed storage was the family's repository for its silver flatware and serving pieces.

95. *(Below)* Detail of the ceiling in the dining room of the Cohen-Bray House. The original wallpaper in the dining room includes some extraordinary and elaborate Aesthetic designs that were probably printed in America.

(Overleaf) 96. Smoking Room of the Cohen-Bray House (1906). Entering this room through the doorway at the left is like stepping from the nineteenth into the twentieth century. This contrast of different worlds was occasioned by the 1906 earthquake, for the remodeling occurred as a result of repairs to a fallen chimney. This new room was created in response to a growing need for an informal, all-purpose living space. The turn of the twentieth century found many Americans ready to embrace greater informality at home. Looking like a room in a vacation lodge or a bungalow, this L-shape space has an uncomplicated, cozy charm that is unusual for a proper Victorian home. The influence of the Arts and Crafts Movement is apparent in the extensive use of redwood, massive structural beams, predominant horizontal lines, flowing open space, and the lantern-hung fireplace. This room survives as a fascinating bridge between two important American periods.

were filled in without covering them up. Some of the finest examples of Stick style in America are of this type.

The so-called Eastlake influence resulted in another version of the Stick style, and it was particularly evident in San Francisco and the Bay Area. The genesis of this new influence was the English writer and tastemaker Charles Locke Eastlake (1836–1906), and largely the result of his trademark book *Hints on Household Taste* (1868), which was considered progressive thinking about domestic furnishings and decoration that reached an enormous audience in America.

Eastlake's book proposed ideas for household furnishings that were based on simple natural materials, sturdy construction, and the honest expression of both; his designs were largely inspired by household furniture forms of the medieval period that were similar to early English Arts and Crafts furniture. In America, the popularity of Eastlake's ideas (at least in theory) was rapid and extensive, and his name soon become a household word. This did not go unnoticed by eager furniture manufacturers. When they began to manufacture "Eastlake furniture," the results were rather far removed from Eastlake's ideas, so most of the mass-produced versions were a meaningless, half-baked pastiche of adapted forms and details. Nevertheless, Americans were fascinated by this furniture probably because it was considered modern. The furniture details that most typified American versions of Eastlake's designs included chamfered or beveled corners and edges, framed insets of diagonal tongue-in-groove paneling, simple incised, or sometimes chip-carved decoration, and fretsawn geometric borders. Small, turned-wood decorations were especially popular as the supports of short rails or galleries that trimmed the tops or shelves of some designs. The interiors of houses sometimes had Eastlake detailing, particularly on their woodwork, such as fireplace mantels, stair railings, and door and window casings.

Eastlake furniture in America came to be synonymous with the taste of the Aesthetic Movement, which was at its peak of influence in the 1880s. Popularized by design-advice books and decorating periodicals, its ideas centered on the idea of merging art with mundane daily living, and the importance of creating thoughtfully designed artistic interiors. Aesthetic taste admired virtually all varieties of Oriental design, particularly that of Japan, and encouraged the collecting of whatever examples one could afford. Japanese prints and fans were favorite accessories, as were porcelain and blue-and-white china, and the motifs of the sunflower and the lily became widely recognized symbols.

Inspired by the elegance of Japanese black-lacquer furniture and objects, much American Eastlake furniture was produced with an ebonized finish, and its incised decorations were often highlighted with gold leaf. This technique was not only applied to all types of furniture, but also to the woodwork of high-style interiors. Indeed, there was virtually no aspect of home design that escaped the possibility of an Eastlake imprint, and Eastlake-style details soon became part of the working vocabulary of many architects, builders, and carpenters in every region of the country, especially in San Francisco and the Bay Area.

Upon hearing about and seeing how his ideas were adapted in America, Charles Eastlake politely but vehemently disclaimed the results. Some members of the local architectural community agreed with him, saying that the new "Eastlake" houses being built in San Francisco were monstrosities. San Francisco architects James E. and George H. Wolfe, editors and publishers of *California Architect and Building News*, were among the most vocal opponents of the local Eastlake craze. They wrote Eastlake and sent him drawings of the "Eastlake" buildings they abhorred. Eastlake expressed "amazement" that there was a style of *architecture* in America that bore his name, which "judging from the specimens I have seen illustrated may be said to burlesque such doctrines of art as I have ventured to maintain." He said he could have "no real sympathy" for the American "architecture and industrial arts" that were products of his influence, which "by all accounts seem to be extravagant and bizarre." But popular taste has a mind of its own, and the Eastlake "aberrations" continued to be built in great numbers. Stick-style buildings were among the first to foster a proto-modern sensibility that some Americans were beginning to assimilate soon after the mid-nineteenth century. An attraction to whatever was new persisted in our national consciousness and was accordingly linked to the Stick and Eastlake styles when they were the latest trends in popular culture. Whatever they may be called, these houses represent some of the liveliest and most inventive surviving domestic carpentry of the Victorian period.

Queen Anne Style
Grand Finale of Victorian Eclecticism

As its name suggests, the Queen Anne style in American architecture—our most eclectic Victorian style—derives from English sources, not only because its namesake was the eighteenth-century British monarch, who reigned between 1702 and 1714, but also because the term was first associated with another Victorian revival style that originated in England. The earliest examples of the Queen Anne style there were loosely based on buildings dating close to the late seventeenth and early eighteenth centuries. Even in England, however, this was far from being a pure revival style, for these buildings also used forms that were derived from much earlier late-medieval or perhaps Tudor or Renaissance period buildings of half-timbered construction. They generally featured red brick walls sometimes dressed in contrasting pale limestone, multi-paned or sometimes leaded and white-painted window sashes, with high compound-gable or hipped roofs sprouting tall chimneys. Sometimes called Queen Anne Revival in England, the style first emerged in the 1860s as a reaction to what was considered the rigidity of the Gothic Revival and Italianate styles that had dominated the first half of the nineteenth century.

Interest in the Queen Anne Revival was partly due to the same group of people that was associated with the Pre-Raphaelite Brotherhood, who counted among their inner circle John Ruskin, Dante Gabriel Rossetti, William Morris, Edward Burne-Jones, and Philip Webb. Of these, the work of architect Philip Webb had some impact on awakening interest in a freer interpretation of past architecture beyond Classicism and the Gothic Revival. He had designed for William Morris the famous Red House of 1859 outside London—a vernacular red-brick building based on the architecture of farm and manor houses in the surrounding countryside of Kent. Although freshly interpreted, the house was infused with its owner's intense longing for the past. For the better part of the next twenty years, English architects and the public fervently embraced the Queen Anne Revival; its

success was assured by the successful assimilation of nationalistic overtones into this style, which reflected some of the "good olde days" of England.

It is helpful to remember that because America followed England's lead in most matters of style and fashion at this time, there was always something of a delayed reaction here in absorbing and adapting what was "cutting edge." Although we adopted many English conventions, their final expression in our cultural melting pot was unpredictable at best. With no other imported style did our absorption and reinvention of it here produce such a surprising American vernacular as with Queen Anne.

The widely published and admired work of English architect Richard Norman Shaw (1831–1912) is most often cited as the primary source of nineteenth-century British Queen Anne influence in America. First published in America by *Building News* in 1871, the first work designed by Shaw to receive major notice by architects here was a large country house in Sussex called Leyes Wood, which was built in 1868. Typical of Shaw's Queen Anne period, Leyes Wood was a rather rambling interpretation of forms derived from late medieval domestic sources that strongly evoked "olde England." The wings of the building were arranged around a courtyard space, and the assemblage of its parts almost resembled an English village. Over a first storey of red brick, second-floor levels were alternately surfaced with patterned terra-cotta tiles and sections of half-timbering. The gables of some second-floor areas also projected outward, and some walls flared out to shed water away from the side of the building; these details were widely adapted in later American versions.

The most famous example of Shaw's influence in America is the 1874 Watts-Sherman house in Newport, Rhode Island. Designed by Henry Hobson Richardson (1838–1886), one of the century's master architects, its design has been often cited as the forerunner of all American Queen Anne houses. Above

97. Design for a Queen Anne-style house (1884). This was published in the influential pattern book *Picturesque California Homes* by West Coast architects Samuel and Joseph C. Newsom, who maintained offices in San Francisco, Oakland, and Los Angeles. Sumptuous compositions like this set a high standard reflected in many of the Bay Area's most luxurious residences of the late nineteenth century. Seen in this illustration are elements that are typical of the Queen Anne style, such as the high hipped roof with cast-iron cresting, the circular corner tower with a conical cap, decorative shingling, and especially the asymmetrical balance of its overall composition. Aesthetic taste is suggested in both the Japanesque "cracked-ice" patterning in the art-glass panels at the top of the windows and in the radiating sunbursts in the tower and the fan shape in the gable over the entrance.

98. Design for a Queen Anne-style house (1887). Classic features of the style, the tall tower and generous open porch (called a "piazza" on its plan) help create the impression of a large house. Despite the implied pastoral setting, this design was narrow enough to fit on some city lots, and was most suitable for a corner site. With only about 800 square feet per floor, the first floor of the plan included a roomy entry/stair hall, parlor, dining room, and kitchen, with three good-sized bedrooms and a full bath on the second floor. Besides the basement, a large attic for expansion space was contained within the hipped and gabled roof. As part of a monthly supplement in the August 1887 issue of *Scientific American— Architects and Builders Edition*, this design was entitled "A Four Thousand Dollar Cottage." By today's standards, it seems too large to qualify as a "cottage," but at that time the term was used more freely; while it might also describe modest single-storey houses, it was generally used for lower-budget house designs. Not only a trade publication but targeted to the general public as well, the magazine helped educate homeowners about the standards and conventions of the building trade. Each issue included an intriguing mix of articles about the latest trends in decorating, furnishing, gardening, and the newest related products.

99. Queen Anne-style house, San Francisco (1909). Incorporating an existing modest structure first acquired in 1879, Charles Katz finally built his dream house thirty years later, by which date its style must have been considered somewhat old-fashioned. During the years spent planning it, perhaps Katz was inspired by similar examples he saw in pattern books and periodicals: the octagonal corner tower, roof line, and flared shingled cap, varied shingle patterns, and art-glass panels that are above the entry and in the front doors. A small second floor octagonal window repeats the tower's shape. Typical of the Edwardian era are the angled divisions of the upper window sash and the horizontal "piano window" to the right of the entry. A popular turn-of-the-century feature, a piano window was usually found in parlors placed above an upright piano and often had an art-glass panel.

a first floor of granite blocks, its shingled walls and half-timbered detailing are composed beneath the sweep of high-pitched gables penetrated by soaring brick chimneys. A drawing of the so-called living hall of the Watts-Sherman house has been attributed to Stanford White, and he was probably also responsible for its imaginative green-and-gold library scheme in which Colonial and Japanese elements were effortlessly combined. The well-preserved house is presently used as a dormitory for Newport's Salve Regina College.

Queen Anne house plans are often noted for the openness of their interior planning, which contributed to their popular perception as being modern houses. A key component in some large houses, an expanded entry or living hall, probably was inspired by the all-purpose medieval great halls of some English manor houses. This term is generally applied to those entry halls that were large enough to be used as expansion

space for the adjoining public rooms. There was often enough room to accommodate some free-standing furniture, and sometimes built-in seating was incorporated at the foot of the stairs or in a bay window. Living halls might have included an inviting fireplace that was sometimes flanked by built-in benches in an alcove called an inglenook.

The added interest and quirks produced by asymmetry are found in the floor plans of most Queen Anne houses. A prominent feature that adds interest to the outside and space to the inside is the room-wide angled bay window, which in combination with the diagonal placement of a corner fire-place often created octagonal rooms. Another characteristic is the lavish use of art glass and fireplace mantels that had over-mantels with mirror-back display shelves supported on deco-ratively turned columns. Doorways between rooms often had fretwork spandrels that were usually supplemented by fabric

93

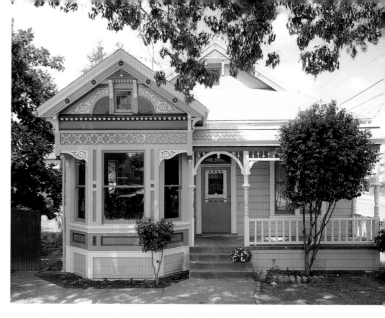

100. *(Opposite)* Queen Anne-style flats, San Francisco (1895). On a prominent uphill corner of the Liberty/Hill Historic District, this towered building was first constructed by contractors Daly and Coldwell. Its form, finish, and details suggest that it may once have been a single-family house. If so, its original character has been more sensitively respected than most houses subjected to later subdivision. Shingles of the "French-cap" roof line and the conical tower have been polychromed to accent their patterns; the tower is crowned by an elegant finial with a gilded and swagged base; fine cast-plaster details, including cherubs with outstretched arms within complex scrollwork, have been strikingly highlighted in gold leaf in frieze panels above the entry and at the bay windows. Other original features include the cast-concrete wall and the partly gilded iron fencing that continues up the stairs.

101. Queen Anne double-row house, San Francisco (1893). In mirror-image fashion, this pair of attached row houses shares every detail in reverse. The expertly creative architect, Henry Geilfuss, did many projects in this neighborhood on the edge of the Western Addition. Spanning the entire width of the lot, a series of strong horizontal elements widen the design and avoid excessive verticality. Angled bays flank a screen-like framework at the center of the first two floors that creates a wide recessed space between them. On the first floor, this forms a double-arched entry portico, and frames unusual front doors with multi-paned windows. Above the portico, a pair of flattened arches, whose upper portions have turned spindlework, frame two original art-glass windows. Above the center of each bay, pairs of large semicircular motifs repeat the double-arch form, and above these are Classical plaster swags that are part of an elaborate frieze that includes spindlework at the outside corners. In the twin gables are small windows adapted from the shape of a Colonial Revival Palladian window.

102. Queen Anne-style cottage, San Leandro, California (c.1895). This charming little house sits close to the ground. It has a hipped roof with a "gable-on-hip" at the center and with an attic window. Sometimes resembling the upper floor and roof of larger Queen Anne houses, such cottages look almost as if they had been lifted off the top of another building. Details typical of this style include the turned "ball-and-stick" fretwork under the porch roof, and the arrangement of paired corner brackets beneath the angled bay window's overhanging gable. The applied cut-out scrollwork in the gable and the geometric frieze below show the complex effects that were easily and economically produced by machines.

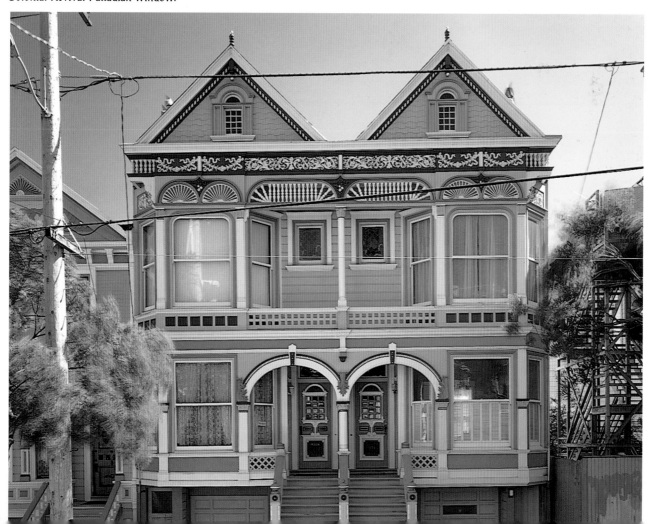

103. Queen Anne row house, San Francisco (1894–1895). Facing Alamo Square, this house was built by developer Matthew Kavanaugh, and today it forms the southernmost end of the famous Postcard Row, centerpiece of the Alamo Square Historic District. Similar in size and plan, the houses on the Row have different detailing and originally cost $3,500 each. Recessed within deep frames, prominent attic-storey gables give the row its distinctive saw-tooth silhouette. Like most Queen Anne compositions, this design fully exploits the effects of light and shadow on its various parts. Gold leaf helps illuminate the Eastlake-influenced bargeboard trim and the grid-like patterning in the gable's recess, where a rounded button at the center of each square reflects light like a miniature sun. A gilded fan becomes a glowing centerpiece above the paired windows. Set to one side, a pediment on top of the entrance portico reproduces the upper gable's detailing in miniature. Original art-glass panels with a shell-and-flower motif have survived in the center window of each bay overlooking Alamo Square.

104. Queen Anne-style row house, San Francisco (c.1895). This imposing Pacific Heights house sits on a graded hillside behind original iron fencing. Like many Queen Anne designs, this has prominent horizontal bands or belt courses that define each floor. The visual weight of the third-storey gable is emphasized by the shadows of its recess and by the simple wide moldings that broaden its eaves. A typical Stick/Eastlake detail is the linear treatment in the gable peak, and beneath the gable is a series of brackets that emphasize the gable's overhang. A delightful Queen Anne accent is the carved and painted panel of stylized sunflowers and foliage between the windows on the right of the second storey.

105. Detail of a front gable on a Queen Anne-style house, San Francisco (1894). This façade's detailing testifies to the skill and imagination of the architect, J.J. Manseau. Beneath projecting gables, angled bay windows trimmed with bracketed corners are typical Queen Anne features, but this one has an unusually elegant composition. Accented by gilded fans at its corners, the three-part central window is the only arched form on the house; opening to the front parlor, its distinctive shape creates a focal point. The floral forms of the frieze on the gable are almost entirely abstracted, and masterfully interpreted in a beautifully carved repeating pattern. The peaked outline of a narrow panel above the frieze is filled with flat-sawn scrollwork. Surrounded by fishscale shingles, the small attic window is framed by brackets supporting a shallow cap; a gilded sunburst complements the carved fans above the central window.

106. Queen Anne-style house, Alameda, California (1889). In an island community near Oakland that is especially noted for its many fine Victorian homes, the design of this house built by architect Charles S. Shaner (who was also its first owner) is quite showy for the building's relatively compact size. The lively contemporary paint scheme creates added drama and whimsy to the overall design and its ornaments. Lacking the large front porch typical of Queen Anne houses in suburban locations, this example has a prominent front portico enriched with carved ornament and a bold pediment above Classical, marbleized columns. The statuesque newel posts at the foot of the front stairs are replacements. A squared bay window makes a pedestal for the round tower that has a supporting bracket in the form of an angel, and a small carved owl is visible at the outside corner of the bay. At the left of the second storey, behind a spindle railing and turned corner post, a diagonal corner window opens onto a shelf-like balcony. Above and between the two center windows, panels of exceptionally complex painted carving are accented in gold leaf. Framed by bargeboards that are decorated with more linear scrolls and stylized floral medallions, the gable's pediment has daintier scrollwork elements arranged around a small attic window. Classical touches appear in the dentil moldings of the roof cornice and in the swagged border encircling the tower just below its conical roof.

107. (Opposite) The Haas-Lilienthal House, San Francisco (1886). On an extra wide lot with a side garden that shows off its remarkable corner tower and complex side elevation to fine advantage, this is a classic example of a large Queen Anne house in an urban context. Its wall textures are varied; the first floor's clapboard siding is the wider "rusticated" type, while a narrower version appears on the second floor; the third floor is then covered in various shingle patterns. Panels of asymmetrical carved, floral motifs accent the upper gables, and circle the tower as part of its frieze. Pediments and finials and a front balcony contribute with the steeply pitched gables to the overall irregular and picturesque massing of the house. William Haas, the prominent merchant who built this house, arrived in San Francisco in 1868, where he prospered in the grocery business. Built for $18,000 (on a $13,000 lot), the house was designed by architect Peter R. Schmidt. Surviving the 1906 earthquake with little damage, the building narrowly escaped the ensuing fire, which was stopped a block to the east at Van Ness Avenue. In 1909, the Haas's daughter Alice was married in the house to Samuel Lilienthal; it was after William Haas died in 1916 that Alice and her husband moved in with Mrs. Haas. Alice lived here until her death in 1972, when the house was donated to the Foundation for San Francisco's Architectural Heritage. Listed on National Register of Historical Places, it is San Francisco Landmark Number 69, and one of two house museums in the City that are open to the public.

108. Detail of the front doors of the Haas-Lilienthal House. The use of sliding-pocket doors for the outer entry was an unusual feature. Tall and paneled, they have beveled-glass panels near the top to admit light into the entry vestibule and entry hall when closed. At that time, open outer doors were a customary symbol of welcome indicating that the family was at home and receiving visitors. A gray marble stairway rises to a pair of low granite posts at the garden level, before continuing up to the covered portico. Although not original, the splendid wrought-iron wall lights were added sometime in the early years of the house.

109. Entry hall and main staircase of the Haas-Lilienthal House. This area was redesigned in 1898, and the update reflects a Classical influence that was then gaining favor. In this view, the glass front doors are at the far end, and show the abundant daylight provided by the open pocket doors; additional light enters through a stairwell window at the left. The main staircase rises between low walls with recessed panels. A survivor of the 1898 remodeling was the elegant newel post light, which was repositioned on one of the low walls. An original fireplace located on the far left wall of this area was removed as part of the remodeling to create a more spacious feeling. Finely finished woodwork of golden quarter-sawn oak is used throughout the area for wainscoting, door casings, and the ceiling cornices.

110. Detail of the entry-hall walls in the Haas-Lilienthal House. This leather-like wallcovering was installed in 1898 above the oak wainscot throughout the entry area. Various sections of the wall covering have elaborate stenciled borders in metallic gold. The border pattern is similar to traditional Celtic-knot designs. The handsome original grandfather clock was made in Germany.

111. Second parlor, looking toward the front parlor of the Haas-Lilienthal House. Capturing the light that streams across the garden on the south side of the house, both of these rooms are spacious and welcoming. Seen in the background, the front parlor's corner bay window is at the base of the tower (see fig. 107). There is a sculptural frieze of highly stylized laurel leaves and berries that is placed below a cornice of both egg-and-dart and dentil moldings. There is a Classical mahogany fireplace mantel enriched by a wide surround of yellow Sienna marble. The room's use of Classical forms reflects the fashionable Beaux Arts influence, and its preference for more academically correct interpretations of historic styles, then rapidly supplanting earlier Victorian eclecticism. In contrast, the second parlor has a less formal feeling. Although its chandelier dates to about the turn of the century, most of this upholstered furniture is of the early twentieth century. An exception is the Rococo Revival-style Belter armchair at the right. In harmony with the deep red of the rare Egyptian Numidian marble fireplace surround, the natural California redwood paneling contributes warmth through its color and grain. The vivid carpet emphasizes the red theme of the room.

(Overleaf) 112. Dining room of the Haas-Lilienthal House. As befits the setting most central to Victorian family life, this room has the most richly realized decorative scheme in the house. The ceiling's height has been tamed by the weight of the impressive grid of beautifully constructed golden-oak box beams. They foreshadow the popularity of box beams in the Edwardian era under the influence of the Arts and Crafts Movement. Now tarnished, the wallcovering originally had a metallic-gold finish and swirling arabesque pattern that was intended to resemble embossed Spanish leather. A combination chandelier of copper and brass designed for both gas and electricity hangs from the center box beam. On the far wall, the built-in sideboard has a mirrored back and glass-fronted cabinets for the Venetian and Bohemian glassware. The custom-made dining table can expand to seat up to twenty people; its chairs were recovered at a later date with finely worked needlepoint designs. A collaborative effort of fifteen family members and friends, the needlework designs repeat the colors and motifs of the carpet. The fireplace mantel displays a gilt-bronze French clock and candelabra set of about 1880 above a surround of dark green Italian marble and strong Classical forms carved of golden oak. The brass andirons are winged griffins. Most likely of redwood, the room's wainscoting was "grained" to match the adjacent oak. Connecting to the second parlor through a large set of pocket doors opposite the fireplace, this room also opens to the entry/stair hall through the door at the right and to the butler's pantry through the door near the corner.

113. Detail of the fireplace in the sitting room of the Haas-Lilienthal House. Made of Mexican onyx, this original fireplace mantel features simplified Classical forms in a design similar to those seen in upscale Italianate-style houses. Most distinctive is the cast-iron fireback, whose raised relief has a repeating motif of sunflowers, a popular symbol of Aesthetic Movement taste. Despite the presence of logs and andirons, it was originally used to burn coal for heat.

114. Master bathroom in the Haas-Lilienthal House. This room was expanded in the 1898 remodeling to allow space for a new bathtub and the dressing-table cabinetry. Porcelain fixtures and nickel-plated plumbing hardware represent the latest in bathroom technology of the time. A durable glazed-ceramic tile wainscot is trimmed by a border with a shell motif. Tubs with enclosed bases like this example were more expensive than the more usual footed variety; another upgrade was the extra-large elliptical pedestal sink with a fluted-column base. To the right of the tub a gas-fired burner was used to provide heat for curling irons. The medicine-cabinet doors are faced with beveled mirrors; over the dressing table, a tall wide mirror is lit by a cleverly mounted wall fixture. Attesting to their enduring appeal, designs very similar to the sink, the large shower head, and the glass shelves with nickel-plated frames are widely reproduced today.

115. Detail of a bathroom in the Haas-Lilienthal House. This unusual wainscot faced with original transfer-printed ceramic tiles survives along with the footed tub in a second-floor bathroom. Inspired by similarly patterned blue-and-white chinaware that was very popular at that time, these stylized floral designs and geometric patterns reflect Aesthetic Movement taste.

116. The John McMullen House, San Francisco (1881; with later additions). Once a row house on a standard lot, this house was completely transformed by several additions and the expansion of its lot. It is one of the City's finest Queen Anne houses. The original owner, John McMullen, came to San Francisco in 1876 from Connecticut. As he became more successful in business he and his wife Lena chose to expand their house, rather than move elsewhere. In 1890, the prominent local architect Samuel Newsom was hired to enlarge the house, and the additions included the front entry's striking horseshoe arch, the large tower at the right, the hipped roof with iron cresting, an extension toward the rear, and new basement rooms. The McMullens continued the process in 1892, when they had the kitchen widened and extended; they bought the adjoining lot to the south by the mid-1890s and added a landscaped garden. Before the turn of the century, another addition of two stories was made to the rear and right side of the house, which resulted in the present distinctive L-shape that embraces the garden, and the grand dining room was probably added at this time. Acquired by its current owners in 1978, it was meticulously restored after a major fire in 1994, and is now operated as a venue for various special events. The McMullen House is listed on the National Register of Historic Places, and is San Francisco Landmark Number 123.

117. Entry hall of the McMullen House (1890). Visitors who pass through the front doors at right enter another world filled with exotic fretwork, colorful patterns, and glowing art glass. Part of the 1890 addition, this room's richly varied components set the tone for the entire house. Because most of the damage caused by the fire in 1994 was to the upper and rear portions of the house, the main public spaces, although damaged by smoke and water, were spared, and all have since been carefully restored. The exceptionally handsome stair railing is made up of elaborately carved panels in two alternating patterns similar to Islamic motifs. The woodwork and inlaid floors are of quartersawn oak. At the right beneath the arch art-glass prisms shower light onto the stair landing and in the circular tower. The art-glass transom and the panel behind the railing are also original. The vibrant handprinted wallpaper patterns are copies or adaptations of period designs.

118. Inside the entry-hall tower of the McMullen House (1890). On a sunny day the interior of this tower becomes a dazzling jewelbox of light and color. The curving built-in bench is a masterful piece of cabinetry. The elaborate chandelier is a restored period fixture.

119. Center parlor of the McMullen House (1890). Revealing part of the building's physical history, this room has two distinct areas. Viewed from the entry hall doorway, the dropped beam that is supported by a single column rising from a built-in circular bench indicates the former location of an outside wall; the area at the left was part of the original 1881 house. A structural necessity, the column with its unusual round seat and bell-shaped back helps combine the two spaces, and the herringbone-pattern floor also unites them. Possibly the original dining room, the area at the left has a glass door leading to the kitchen, which is still in its original location. The tall built-in china cabinet matches the room's mahogany woodwork. The corner fireplace has an overmantel with a beveled mirror, slender columns supporting an upper shelf, and a carved top. The original copper-plated fittings for the coal-burning firebox remain in place. The surround's green-glazed tiles frame a ceramic plaque with a reclining figure. A wide single pocket door opens to the breakfast room, and beyond it is the dining room at the back of the house. A stylized 1870s lily pattern designed by American architect P.B. Wight is in the handprinted wallpaper.

120. Dining room of the McMullen House (c.1898). This generously scaled room forms the short end of the L-shape that the house acquired after the rear addition was made. Through the doorway we see the adjoining breakfast room and on into the center parlor. A single door to the right of the art-glass window in the breakfast room opens into the garden. Adapted from a period frieze by British designer Walter Crane, a serpentine design of peacocks enlivens the wallpaper in the coved ceiling. Beneath them is an ornate pattern inspired by the work of William Morris. With the exception of the Regency-style pedestal sideboard at the far left, the dining-room furniture is reproduced from eighteenth-century designs, thus reflecting Colonial Revival taste.

portières. Wide doorways fitted with sliding pocket doors were another popular feature in Queen Anne floor plans, thus emphasizing the concept of more flowing interior spaces.

Among the most characteristic exterior features of American Queen Anne houses is the use of complex hipped roofs, and one of its most definitive forms is the tower, which was usually placed at a corner. The typical round Queen Anne tower with a conical roof is a French medieval form. The sides of towers were generally either round or multi-sided—usually octagonal, but rarely square. Bell-shaped towers were popular with adventuresome architects and were also illustrated in many pattern books. Prominent front porches are another important part of American Queen Anne houses. The shadows and roof lines were frequently employed to picturesque effect; sometimes porches were extended to wrap around the house, and provided convenient places to display a multitude of fancily turned posts, often with lacy spandrels stretching between them. The use of machine-carved wooden ornaments reached its apex in the Queen Anne style, and the shapes and combinations provided endless variety.

Whimsy, one of the most charming characteristics of the Queen Anne style, would eventually prove to be the most convenient target for criticism of it. After the legendary triumph of Beaux Arts classicism that was so sweepingly demonstrated by the White City of Chicago's 1893 World's Columbian Exposition, the days of the Queen Anne style were numbered. Increasingly perceived as the style of hopelessly impractical "white elephants" after only a decade or two, the Queen Anne was the last gasp of Victorian eclecticism.

121. Falkirk (The Robert Dollar Mansion), San Rafael, California (1888). Although it is now most associated with shipping magnate Robert Dollar (and later named for his birthplace in Scotland), this house was first built for Ella Nichols Park, who hired prominent San Francisco architect Clinton Day to design it. Falkirk's rambling design influenced by the half-timbered English Tudor style incorporates numerous gables and dormers in a deliberately asymmetrical composition. Sited up a gentle hillside, it overlooks rolling lawns, mature trees, and a large lily pond. This picturesque building was created with such diverse building materials as stucco, stone, brick, shingles, and wood siding. The entrance is recessed within the deep overhang of the front porch. At the left, a tower's angled bays anchor the outside corner of the library and a bedroom above.

122. Detail of façade of Falkirk. Painted to repeat the red of the brick chimney, the deeply carved decorative panel above the porch roof is probably the façade's most refined detail. Inspired by old European buildings, Queen Anne-style compositions like this were a fully calculated effort by the architects, who arranged the elements to look as if construction had occurred in phases over a long period.

123. Art-glass panels that light the stairwell of Falkirk.

(Overleaf) 124. Entry hall of Falkirk. Appropriately placed at the heart of the home, a massive fireplace commands the center of attention in this spacious "living" hall. Half-fluted, overscaled columns support a thick, outward-curving shelf, on which a series of delicate columns and matching pilasters create display spaces. Admitting light to the area is a large art-glass panel that extends to the second floor. The handsome paneled wainscot, which extends up the stairwell, is made of Sierra pine and redwood with burled ash at the center of each panel. The beamed and paneled ceiling is made entirely of California redwood. At the far end, pocket doors have been opened to the dining room. A glass door at the right leads to a small solarium, which also connects with the dining room and to the garden.

125. Parlor of Falkirk. The most magnificent room in the house, the parlor has an exceptional all-redwood vaulted ceiling. Ideal for music recitals, the room has superb acoustics that are enhanced by its shape and finish. The massive fireplace of the entry hall is visible through the wide doorway; the open doorway in the entry hall leads to the back hall containing the servants' stairs. The two large portraits are of the best-known previous residents, Mr. and Mrs. Robert Dollar, who acquired the house in 1906 from the estate of Ella Nichols Park for $26,500. After being threatened with demolition in 1972, the house was saved by the efforts of Marin Heritage and then acquired by the city of San Rafael. Today, it is operated as the multi-functional Falkirk Cultural Center and is open to the public.

126. The George W. Patterson House, Fremont, California (1889). An excellent example of the Queen Anne style, this house is situated in a grove of mature trees. A simple 1857 farmhouse was substantially enlarged and restyled to its present appearance in 1889 by George W. Patterson, and was the centerpiece of a prosperous cattle ranch he called Arden. Patterson's son had the dining room remodeled in the Craftsman style in 1915. Most of the original interiors and furnishings of the house remain intact. Emphasized by the shadows of the porches are graceful arches, most notably the arch of the main entrance with its monumental sweep. The tower at the left has a very unusual mosaic frieze below the eaves. The covered porch at the right with Colonial Revival-style columns was a later addition. The Patterson House and its 205-acre site have been carefully preserved to reflect the daily lives of both the owners and the employees of a nineteenth-century ranch and its evolution into the twentieth century. The place is open to the public under the name of Ardenwood Regional Park.

127. Gazebo of the Patterson House. Set across the lawn from the house, this gazebo provides a shady spot to admire the grounds. The design of its posts, rails, and the lattice-like screens of its spandrels and cupola are adapted from elements found on the house. Screened by the vegetation behind it is an access road leading to nearby outbuildings.

128. The Riddell-Fish House, Benicia, California (c.1890). Strikingly framed between a pair of towering palms, this house is a study in asymmetrical architecture. Built for Mr. and Mrs. Franklin Fish, the house is documented by surviving original floor plans and family photos. Henrietta Riddell Fish was a noted local artist known to have exhibited paintings at the 1915 Panama-Pacific International Exposition in San Francisco. Although it is situated near the center of Benicia, its enormous lot and mature landscaping have kept neighboring houses at a distance, and preserved some of its original rural atmosphere. Although it does not have a large front porch, the house has an otherwise characteristic Queen Anne design with an irregular hipped roof, a round corner tower, and patterned shingles in the upper storeys. Typically eclectic is the combination of Eastlake influence in the linear geometric detailing and the Palladian window set into the upper gable, a form most associated with Colonial Revival houses. Alterations made in the mid-1930s included enclosing a second-floor balcony to make the bay window at the right and the addition of the horizontal windows above the front porch.

Colonial Revival/Classical Revival Styles
American Nationalism and the Beaux Arts Influence

Considering its appearance and influence, the Colonial Revival was a kind of cleansing mechanism for public taste toward the end of the nineteenth century. The earliest known date for its influence is the early 1870s, but Americans attending the 1876 Centennial Exposition in Philadelphia would have been among the first to be clearly influenced, for the Exposition is generally considered to be the start of the Colonial Revival in America.

The exhibits at Philadelphia in 1876 extolled our glorious first century and provided the fairgoers with an overview of America's founding and of its most famous places and players. The Exposition also displayed the latest major advances of industry and technology together with a dizzying array of products and architecture from many foreign lands. An important result of the Exposition was the realization that the concept of selling America on its own history cannot be underestimated. Timing certainly had a lot to do with the concept; once America hit one hundred years of age, there was a widespread, grass-roots reaction throughout the country that there were certain parts of our early history to study, preserve, collect, or perhaps emulate. Nationalism had come of age in America, and many of our citizens were eager to find ways to express it.

For the first time, American architecture, furniture, and other decorative arts (typically of the eighteenth-century Georgian period leading up to our Revolution) were being rediscovered and reassessed. The first collections of early American furniture were established soon after this time. An awareness of the importance of preserving our rapidly vanishing early historic houses and other important historic sites (particularly those associated with key events or the "founding fathers") was widely discussed and slowly began to be implemented. Because the world had so changed, and the country had so exploded in growth and industry, legendary names of our past like Washington, Franklin, Jefferson, Adams (and even Betsy Ross) became new household words in a way they never were in the eighteenth century. In this atmosphere, inevitably, new domestic architecture, interior design, and decorative arts could not escape Colonial influence.

If it took a while after the 1876 Exposition for domestic architecture to begin to reflect the Colonial Revival influence, some pioneering architectural work had already been done that has been cited as its earliest-known example. The year was 1872, the architect was Charles Follen McKim (1847-1909), and the place was Newport, Rhode Island. He is best known as one of the partners of the prominent New York architectural firm of McKim, Mead and White. McKim had studied at the Ecole des Beaux Arts in Paris and also had a useful background in engineering. In the early 1870s, he was living in Newport, and had undertaken the remodeling of an eighteenth-century house on Washington Street. Among the innovative changes he made was to remodel the original kitchen at the back of the house into an informal living room, so as to enjoy the view overlooking the water. The large original kitchen fireplace was retained, but McKim redesigned its mantel and the surrounding new paneling to recall elements of the woodwork and original detailing he admired in the formal rooms.

In 1874, Charles McKim's early Colonial Revival efforts were photographed and published in the *New York Sketchbook of Architecture,* which was mostly a visual exploration of surviving eighteenth-century buildings (some in varying states of picturesque disrepair). McKim was also an assistant editor of this book, and that is another reason why he deserves much of the credit for the beginnings of the Colonial Revival movement. This book also awakened an awareness of the Shingle style, for some of the historic buildings shown were of the "shingle vernacular," certainly an important

129. Kentucky Building, World's Columbian Exposition, Chicago, Illinois (1893). In keeping with the famous event's theme, this Classical Revival building also shows Colonial Revival elements. Designed by architects Maury and Dodd of Louisville, it was described as "Southern colonial architecture" and was illustrated in a hardcover souvenir book, *The Columbian Exposition Album.* Built at a cost of $18,000, it measured 75 by 95 feet. Monumental fluted Ionic columns are combined with pilasters against the front walls; above a plain frieze, the cornice incorporates dentil molding that also frames the pediment. A semicircular columned porch is at the right. A rounded two-storey bay window rises through it, topped by a curving balcony that is echoed by the railing at the roof level. Window casings recall a Greek Revival form. A Chinese Chippendale fretwork railing on the hipped roof, turned-spindle balusters, swagged-plaster decoration, a fanlight transom, and a Palladian window are Colonial Revival features. Inside were three large rooms for the exhibition of local industry and art, plus dining rooms, smoking rooms, libraries, and retiring rooms. Instead of renderings like this, most of the book's images were actual photographs; this one may have been taken from a preliminary presentation drawing. The statue of the state's frontier luminary Daniel Boone is by Louisville's Enid Yandell.

130. Colonial revival-style house, San Francisco (c.1907). With a correct and prim posture that appears to have been imported from New England, this house in the Presidio Heights district was designed by architect William Bliss for Mr. and Mrs. E. J. Bowen. It is not an academic copy of a Colonial house, but rather a sensitive interpretation by the architect. The beautifully detailed and proportioned elements include a fine cornice and pediment, a split fanlight attic window, divided-light window sash, shuttered second-floor windows, and narrow wood siding. Its columned recessed entry vestibule has a segmental arched pediment. To avert the possibility of an obtrusive house at the right, Mrs. Bowen had the Bliss and Faville firm design one for that site, which was built in 1909 to complement this house.

131. Colonial Revival-style house, San Francisco (1896). There is a dignified repose about this Haight-Ashbury district house that highly commends the abilities of its architect, Edward J. Vogel. In its fairly constricted urban lot, Vogel created a light, freestanding, and captivating design. The placement and proportion of every element and detail have been carefully conceived and finely carried out. A subtle contrast of texture plays between the smoothness of the first-floor walls and the horizontal lines of the narrow wood siding above. The elegance of the semicircular portico is beautifully complemented by that of the bay window. Small balconies above both portico and bay are enclosed by delicately spindled railings used with robust turned posts. Arching fanlight transoms above the second-storey windows reflect the bowed forms below them. Rising from the hipped roof are beautifully detailed attic dormers with diamond-paned sash. The two-storey pilasters at the outside corners emphasize the height and also add an element of grandeur to the house. The slanted bay window on the side façade has an arching fanlight that matches those on the front. Circular windows set within plaster wreaths are set at the left and right of the windows on the side. Classical swags, ribbons, and wreaths enliven the attic gables, large upper frieze, and the tops of the portico and bay windows. The strongly horizontal water-table line around the top of the basement level anchors the vertical lines of the house to the ground.

132. *(Left)* The McCreary-Greer House, Berkeley, California (c.1901). One of the finest Colonial Revival-style houses of the East Bay, this house is a stately presence in Berkeley's early College Homestead neighborhood. Its most commanding feature is the commodious front porch with its roof partly enclosed by a boldly scaled Classical railing and supported by groups of Ionic columns. Typical of the Colonial revival style are the Palladian window of the parlor at the right and the oval window at the center of the second floor, both of which retain original art glass. The origin of this house is unclear; it may have been designed as early as 1896 by Cornelius S. McNally, or possibly by Barker Estey in 1901. The house was acquired in 1907 by J. Edward McCreary, who was in the oil business. His family continued to occupy it until 1981, when neighborhood resident Ruth Alice Greer purchased it to ensure its preservation. In 1986, she donated the house to the Berkeley Architectural Heritage Association, an active preservation group; it is now their headquarters.

133. *(Below)* Colonial Revival-style house, San Francisco (1896). What corner houses may lack in garden space, they certainly make up in visibility. Although shallow in depth, the width is equivalent to several row houses. Designed by architect W.H. Lillie, the house enjoys outlooks across the street to the verdant slopes of Alta Plaza. The immediate area is a microcosm of San Francisco's residential development since the 1870s, for elegant homes face Alta Plaza on all sides. Centered on the symmetrical façade is an engaged entry portico with paired Ionic columns and a recessed vestibule. Above it, a shallow bay of unusual swelling form incorporates a Palladian window. Supported by curving brackets, angled bay windows at the left and right repeat the balcony effect seen above the portico. The projections of the frieze above each bay contribute to the lively effect of its cast-plaster design. Considered a signature of the architect, the same intertwining pattern of Classical swags, wreaths, and torches appears on several of his projects.

134. Detail of façade of a Colonial Revival-style house (1897). Opposite Buena Vista Park in the Haight-Ashbury district, this house was designed by architect Edward J. Vogel for Floyd Spreckles, a member of a prominent local family. Although of a grander scale, its design is closely related to another house by the same architect a few blocks away (see fig. 131). The semicircular portico above marble steps has pairs of Ionic columns and a cast-plaster frieze of wreaths and swags that is repeated in the frieze below the cornice. The handsome windows are highlighted with elaborate fanlights and delicate plaster relief ornament. Local legend suggests that the spacious attic floor of this house was occupied for a time by famous turn-of-the-century authors Ambrose Bierce and Jack London.

135. Classical Revival house, San Francisco (1897). On a hillside facing east just below Alamo Square, this stunning house was built for John L. Koster, president of the California Barrel Company, who was also proprietor of the Mount Hamilton Vineyard. One of the most imposing residences in the Alamo Square Historic District, it was designed by the firm of Martens & Coffey. In order to encompass the expansive views, each corner was extended outward into a rounded tower-like bay from the foundation to the roof. Prominent arched hoods above the first-floor windows have elaborate plaster decorations with a shell motif. Up a flight of stairs, entry is through the side of a dramatic portico with Ionic columns, and the portico's projection creates semicircular balconies on two levels. Pairs of engaged Corinthian columns, which appear layered on top of pilasters behind them, rise for two storeys. At the center of the second floor a shallow-bowed bay window opens onto the spacious balcony. There is a typical oval window in the central pediment, and one of the arch-topped dormers on the hipped roof is visible. Although they often share features and detailing with Colonial Revival houses, Classical Revival houses like this example generally have grander proportions, and often feature two-storey porticos with equally monumental columns and pilasters.

136. Classical Revival house, San Francisco (1895). An elegant design made more imposing by its uphill site, this Pacific Heights house was designed by prominent local architect A. Page Brown (1859–1896). Its design gains from a spare use of ornament, and its impact relies on a strong sense of composition and scale. Each floor of the house is clearly defined by horizontal belt courses. The attic level probably included servants' quarters. The façade's focal point is the graceful bow-front portico with Ionic columns and the three-part Palladian window above, with the divided arched sash that recalls the eighteenth-century Gothick style. A. Page Brown is best-remembered today as the designer of the Beaux Arts-influenced Ferry Building in San Francisco. After training at Cornell, he worked as a draftsman for the great New York firm of McKim, Mead and White before coming to San Francisco in 1889.

(Overleaf) 137. Dunsmuir House, Oakland, California (1899). In a sheltered meadow at the foot of the East Bay hills, this stunning house is a rare survivor. Designed by architect J. Eugene Freeman, this great example of the Classical Revival style of over 16,000 square feet has thirty-seven rooms, and has attic-level quarters for twelve live-in staff. Important for grand country-house entertainments, living space could be expanded by the extensive covered verandas. When built, the porte cochère could have sheltered either a horse-drawn carriage or an early automobile. This house was built for Alexander Dunsmuir, the second son of Robert Dunsmuir of Victoria, British Columbia, an immigrant Scotsman and wealthy coal baron. In 1878, he was sent to the Bay Area to run the family-owned Wellington Colliery. He joined the local high life, where he met and courted a married woman named Josephine Bower Wallace. She was able to divorce her husband amicably and moved in with Alexander together with her daughter Edna. However, his powerful mother's opposition to their marriage delayed it for nearly two decades. Finally, a family agreement was reached, and just prior to their wedding, Alexander had this house built for Josephine. But he became ill on their honeymoon in New York and died there. Josephine died soon after in 1901. Meanwhile, Edna had grown up to become Edna Wallace Hopper, a then-famous Broadway stage star. She inherited Dunsmuir House from her mother, but didn't have the resources to support it. I. W. Hellman, Jr. of Wells Fargo Nevada National Bank and his family bought it in 1906, and they were the last private owners of the estate they called Oakvale Park. Acquired by the City of Oakland for a conference center site in 1962, Dunsmuir House was designated a National Historic Site in 1972, and an Oakland Landmark in 1980, and today it is open to the public.

aspect of American Colonial architecture. Rediscovery of shingled buildings as a creative vehicle for a new domestic architecture was soon to have far-reaching effects.

As Colonial Revival architecture began to appear more routinely in the 1880s, there was the challenge of how historically accurate it should, or needed to, be. This consideration was certainly more pointed for architects like Charles McKim, who had the training and background to know the difference. For many architects it was refreshing to work in a style that seemed more orderly and formulaic than the rather freewheeling versions of historic revivalism that had taken up much of the nineteenth century. By comparison, the forms and motifs of classicism were perceived (not always correctly) as essentially a language that could be learned by following conventions and rules to create a plausible design.

If the 1876 Exposition in Philadelphia was considered the inaugural event of the Colonial Revival style, then the 1893 World's Columbian Exposition in Chicago was in many ways its launching pad (if not its apogee). Most of the principal buildings were grandly vast and reflected the gleaming, rigidly Classical Beaux Arts approach favored by most of the participating architects; it was nicknamed "The White City." An international event, there were also buildings in many different styles from around the world.

Various American states participated in the fair by erecting smaller structures in styles mostly inspired by Colonial Revival taste. Probably it was considered the most appropriate style for an event that was envisioned as a rallying point for cultural and political nationalism. Many of the state buildings with their grandly columned porticoes are probably better described as Classical Revival. This event was and is considered a watershed of American architectural taste. Its blinding whiteness was dazzling and fresh to the fairgoers, and many, including most of the participating architects, thought it was a real vision of the future for American cities. Fairs over the next two decades copied the Beaux Arts style and planning of the Chicago fair, notably at Buffalo in 1901, St. Louis in 1904, and San Francisco in 1915.

A prominent dissenting voice to all the Beaux Arts grandeur was that of Louis Henri Sullivan (1856–1924), a great Chicago architect who was also mentor to Frank Lloyd Wright. Sullivan designed the enormous Transportation Building at the Exposition; it was not in the prevailing Beaux Arts taste. Sullivan felt that the 1893 fair was the death knell of a true American architecture, created on our soil and without the flagrantly European influences of the Beaux Arts style.

However, the 1893 Exposition was a moment of great national pride, and had made an architectural statement perfectly expressing this sentiment. After viewing the fair, prominent citizens of wealth and power across America were inspired to enhance our cityscapes with projects that enriched civic pride and spread the message of patriotism; typical was the commissioning of large commemorative fountains and statues. Museums, universities, and important public buildings were also founded or constructed with private monies.

More than at any other time, it was a period when America's rich "gave back" in ways that patronized the arts, especially through public architecture. From 1876 to about the time of World War I, this period of artistic idealism and public expressions of America's greatness has been aptly described as the American Renaissance.

The overall planning of the 1893 World's Columbian Exposition was under the direction of the notable American architect Daniel Burnham. He was already well known for his work with the Chicago firm of Burnham & Root, a part of the progressive Chicago School. They were prominent enough to handle projects elsewhere in the country; their still-intact 1892 Mills Building in downtown San Francisco at Bush and Montgomery Streets was an early skyscraper in the Romanesque Revival style that survived the 1906 earthquake and fire. Burnham also became a leading city planner, and was a well-known advocate of the City Beautiful movement. An outgrowth of Beaux Arts ideals, it wanted to reorganize the haphazard growth of American cities into more coherent and elegant compositions of wide boulevards and axial vistas with grand complexes of civic buildings. Nationwide interest in the idea evolved as a direct result of the success of the 1893 Exposition. Burnham actually prepared plans for the makeover of parts of Chicago and a major reworking of San Francisco's plan, but little happened. Only San Francisco's plan had a fighting chance after the destruction of 1906 cleared so much land, but local politics defeated the idea, and the City was rebuilt on its old grid. However, the stunning Beaux Arts civic center of San Francisco is considered the finest example in America of a grand urban complex built to the City Beautiful ideal.

This chapter is illustrated by examples of houses that are identified by two style names: both Colonial Revival- and Classical Revival-style houses are contemporaneous and created with similar classical architectural forms and details. The style names help distinguish their chief differences, which are primarily those of scale. Houses in the Colonial Revival style are generally of relatively modest proportions, but this style was broadly interpreted with wide variety as a result. It was popularized as a style of chaste and classical forms that were considered tasteful replacements for the excessive ornamentation of Queen Anne and earlier Victorian houses. The style has been very durable, extending well past World War I into the 1920s and beyond, although later examples of the style look quite different from those built before 1900. Even with the advent of the Modern movement the Colonial Revival did not perish, for it remains today as the most popular domestic architectural style in our history.

The Classical Revival style was far more unusual because it was reserved for mansions. It is easily recognized by the frequent use of a classically columned, two-storey, temple-front portico and tall pilasters, which are flattened columnar forms attached to the wall. Not every Classical Revival design has a two-storey portico, for some are composed with two-storey pilasters and a single-storey portico, which is more an exception than a rule. Compared to most Colonial Revival-style

138. Entry hall of Dunsmuir House. What strikes most visitors is the wonderful spaciousness of this area, typical of a house that was designed for entertaining, and somewhat similar to a living hall in a large Queen Anne house. Although open and flowing, this room has different areas that are defined by its architecture; the large dropped beam at the center designates its two primary zones. In the front area, a fireplace (out of view at the left) is placed on an angled wall and is part of a seating alcove with windows on two sides (one can be seen at the left). Colonial Revival taste is signified by the Classical woodwork details and the delicate divisions of the fanlight transom and sidelights of the wide front entrance. The patterned hardwood floors are an original feature that vary in each room. Through the open doorway with pocket doors is a large parlor. Lighted from above by a large art-glass dome (see fig. 142), the main staircase rises from the landing at right in the back area of the entry hall. An extensive use of box beams here and in most of the other public rooms was fashionable at that time. Although not original here, the use of white painted woodwork was to become popularly associated with the Colonial Revival style. Most of the interior wall finishes are not original to the house; some, like the painted finish on these walls, remain from set decorations made for various movies that have been filmed here. However, most of the building's important original features are well preserved. The mahogany hall bench at the far left is the only surviving piece of furniture that belonged to Alexander Dunsmuir.

designs, they tend to be more formal, symmetrical, and almost sober in character. To some extent there are parallels in the scale and massing of some Classical Revival houses to that of the earlier columned and temple-fronted houses of the Greek Revival, and they can be sometimes confused.

While fairly well represented here, Colonial Revival is not a common Victorian Bay Area style; it is far more prevalent in the East and Midwest. Most local examples feature balanced, but asymmetrical compositions, routinely embellished with decorative friezes or other ornaments in Classical forms of delicate cast plaster. A hipped roof with dormers is one of the most usual features of local examples. Colonial Revival interiors generally have details that repeat some of the Classical motifs on the exteriors, such as columns, turned balusters, spindles, and dentil and other moldings. Often used in two tiers, columns were used on fireplace mantels to support the

main shelf and an overmantel with a beveled mirror and upper display shelf. Ceilings were frequently coved and box beams were also a common feature.

Colonial Revival furniture looked quite different from most of the previous Victorian styles. Especially after 1900, its fashionable presence made earlier pieces seem increasingly outdated. A subject of serious study after gaining attention at the 1876 Philadelphia Exposition, America's eighteenth-century furniture styles were routinely copied by manufacturers, and many adaptations flooded American parlors. Sets of department-store dining furniture vaguely Colonial in style was found in countless middle-class homes.

As a decorating style, Colonial Revival was probably even more popular than it was for architecture, and its influence dominated most decorating periodicals just before 1900 and long after. It proved to have far longer staying power than any

139. Dining room of Dunsmuir House. Entered from the rear area of the entry hall, this room's highlight is the wonderful built-in cabinetry and wainscot paneling in dark-stained quartersawn oak. Large beveled mirrors envelop the fireplace wall and shine in the enormous built-in sideboard at the right. Handcarved details in Classical motifs abound on the sideboard; on the lower cabinet doors are beribboned wreaths and the frieze of swags and ribbons across the top is repeated on the fireplace wall. The Hellman family added the German silver chandelier suspended from the box-beam ceiling. The dining room's table and chairs, while not original, date to about the same period as the house.

previous style of the entire nineteenth century. Although most people's homes still had various Victorian pieces passed down through their family, these were usually prized for sentimental reasons rather than their design or monetary value. Some Victorian furniture was painted to look more Colonial, and then might have been used to furnish a spare bedroom. This practice was most common in the 1920s, when it was also used to brighten the dark wood of much Arts and Crafts furniture that had fallen from favor. Two of the most popular symbols of America's Colonial past were the tall-case or so-called grandfather clock that was often placed on a stair landing or somewhere in the entry hall, and the spinning wheel, which was more prized for its atmospheric effect than for any practical use.

It is the very American quality of the Colonial Revival that makes it the one Bay Area style that most resembles its counterparts elsewhere in the country. Perhaps it was the local Victorian-era tradition for the unusual to be found in earlier styles that was a contributing factor to its relative scarcity.

140. Game room of Dunsmuir House. The least formal of the public rooms, this was originally designed to hold a billiard table. Made of California redwood, the high paneled wainscot and box-beam ceiling are very simply detailed. Partly seen at the right is the fireplace, faced in carved brick and terra-cotta; the padded fender in front of it is for extra seating. Through the wide doorway is the parlor with an outstanding architectural mahogany mantel, fluted Classical columns, and friezes carved with wreath and ribbon motifs. The inlaid games table and high-backed chairs might well be "Grand Tour" souvenirs, for they are typical of the French reproductions of antique styles that were favored at the time by America's well-to-do.

141. Library of Dunsmuir House. Situated near the area of the rear entry hall, this room has an informal, cozy quality. On the wall opposite the doorway is a large semicircular bay window seen at the right side of figure 137. Built-in glass-fronted bookcases matching those in the far corner also line the wall opposite the fireplace. Probably a European import, the handsomely carved marble fireplace mantel was added later by Mrs. Hellman. Although not an original finish, the wallcovering in this room is the earliest of any surviving in the house. The library was also used by men as a smoking room.

142. Gallery (second-floor stairhall) of Dunsmuir House. This intricately worked art-glass dome, also visible from the first floor, is a major focal point of the house. About ten feet in diameter, it is made up of almost seven thousand individual pieces of glass. It also provided plenty of light for this area, which was used as an art gallery. The dome is off-center in the coved ceiling, and it is lit from a skylight at the center of the roof, and also from additional windows on two sides of its third-floor room. This view highlights the Colonial Revival detailing of the stair railing and newel posts.

143. Guest bedroom of Dunsmuir House. The high coved ceilings throughout this floor ensure its open and airy feeling. There are two additional windows to the right of the bed here. Although the wallpaper was a later addition, its pale coloring fits in with the period idea that bedroom decor should be lighter than the public rooms. The "bamboo" spindlework bed and dressing chest dates to the Aesthetic Movement of the 1880s. The diagonal corner placement of the coal-burning fireplace was also common to many Queen Anne houses. While the two-tier mantel shows Classical detailing, it was probably a ready-made stock design. However, a feature that is far more luxurious than the decor is the private bathroom for this room, which can be seen through the door on the far wall, and is illustrated in figure 144. A great luxury for that period, private bathrooms accompany all the other primary bedrooms in Dunsmuir.

144. Guest bathroom in Dunsmuir House. The generous size of this bathroom is comparable to that of a small bedroom, and it is beautifully lit by two windows. Differences between this and other bathrooms in the house suggest that it was remodeled by the Hellmans after 1907. In the 1910s, the pedestal sink with a fluted Classical-column base, the built-in medicine cabinet flanked by a pair of sconces, the toilet with the wall-mounted tank, the glass-rod towel bars (and other hardware) would have all been up-to-date fittings. An innovation that made cleaning easier was the enclosed pedestal-tub base, a newer and more expensive alternative to the usual footed tubs.

145. Tub in the master bathroom of Dunsmuir House. This bath became Mrs. Hellman's part of a His and Hers master bath in their remodel that added another bathroom next to this for Mr. Hellman. Set on a marble splash slab inset into the tile floor, this huge cast-iron tub is an original fixture. The tub's oversized diagonal ball-and-claw feet were engineered to support its great weight. Inspired by the tile border above the tub, delicate swags and ribbons were hand-painted in blue on the tub's sides.

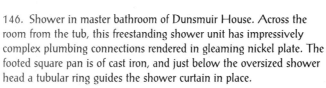

146. Shower in master bathroom of Dunsmuir House. Across the room from the tub, this freestanding shower unit has impressively complex plumbing connections rendered in gleaming nickel plate. The footed square pan is of cast iron, and just below the oversized shower head a tubular ring guides the shower curtain in place.

147. Rib-cage shower in a master bathroom of Dunsmuir House. So described for its skeletal form, this so-called rib-cage shower is in a new bathroom added in the 1910s for Mr. Hellman. Its unique design allowed water to fall from an oversized shower head near the ceiling, and also to spray out horizontally from the encircling tubular "ribs." All of the plumbing hardware and the frame of the glass shower door are nickel-plated.

148. Kitchen stove in Dunsmuir House. This remarkable survivor had to be large, for as many as twenty people a day, including servants, had to be fed. It was designed to burn both wood and coal, and while still in working order, it would take about six hours (starting cold) for the oven to heat up properly for baking. The stove was later converted to gas, including a gas broiler. The kitchen has its original ceramic-tile wainscot and vintage linoleum. At left is the door leading to the servants' dining room; another open door in the far corner leads to the pastry pantry, with a marble slab for rolling dough and built-in bins for flour and sugar.

Shingle Style

Toward Simplicity and the First Bay Tradition

Part of a pivotal new movement in design that emerged near the end of the nineteenth century, the Shingle style for a time became the reason for the development of some of the most progressive and inventive architecture of the late Victorian era. Although it didn't have the same popularity as the Queen Anne and Colonial Revival styles, its beginnings were concurrent with them, and all were quite closely interrelated. Especially in its earlier examples, the Shingle style routinely shared some forms and planning concepts with the Queen Anne, but its detailing was often related to the Colonial Revival; in some ways the Shingle style was a more progressive outgrowth of the latter.

Among the basic characteristics of the Shingle style were simplicity of materials and building plans. Its debt to the Queen Anne style is a significant one, sharing its opened-up floor plans, nontraditional room shapes, and sometimes spacious and flexible living halls. Although typically expressed in overtly decorative ways that put ornamental value above mere textural effects, the Queen Anne style made a signature use of shingles. Among its most typical components, multiple shingle patterns were an integral part of a Queen Anne's vitality.

What initially endeared the Queen Anne style to architects was the sense of a new design freedom it engendered, and the same attraction was true of the Shingle style. Both suggested something new, different, and full of creative possibility. Probably because it was derived from Classical forms, the Colonial Revival movement lacked much spontaneity and whimsy, and generally had a more disciplined approach to its composition and ornament. However, some aspects of the Colonial Revival were successful ingredients of the Shingle style, particularly the recognition of shingled buildings as part of our Colonial past. As the continuation of a worthy tradition, this association shaped the public's image of the Shingle style and secured its future.

Considered the birthplace of the Shingle style, New England was where one could find innumerable examples of antique shingled houses. Their reassessment was in part inspired by the publication of the *New York Sketch Book of Architecture,* which in 1874 documented various Colonial buildings in new photographs. Charles McKim was closely involved with this publication, and one of the photographs that was pivotal to him showed the Bishop Berkeley House (c. 1729) in Middletown, Rhode Island. The photograph of the back of the house revealed a haphazard assemblage of shingled additions under a long, sloping, and slightly sagging shingled roof. This extended, asymmetrical "saltbox" shape is seen on many early New England houses, and is typical of that vernacular architecture. In McKim's opinion, these early Colonial forms were as worthy of emulation as Classical columns, porticoes, and Palladian windows. Subsequently, some of the architecture produced by the firm of McKim, Mead and White after 1879 had similar long, spreading roofs. Also, it is clear that the Bishop Berkeley House inspired Shingle-style designs by other architects.

By the later 1880s, the Colonial Revival movement had become increasingly important, and the Shingle style was developed by such architects as William Ralph Emerson, Lamb and Rich, Arthur Little, Peabody and Stearns, Bruce Price, Henry Hobson Richardson, and John Calvin Stevens, and their work was illustrated in periodicals like *American Architect and Building News* and *American Builder.*

The Shingle style was enduringly popular on the East Coast because it was close to the sources that had inspired it and was comfortably familiar. Most at home in settings in or near seaside resorts in New England, it was also found on Long Island in New York and on the New Jersey shore. Many of these buildings are classics of American domestic architecture, for the complex and rambling compositions wrapped in shingles became remarkably unified and attractive.

The Shingle style in the Bay Area was slow to take off, and never became as widespread as its early proponents had hoped. However, by the 1890s, significant examples had

149. Design for a Shingle-style house (1900). This drawing of a classic Shingle-style house appeared in the October 1900 issue of a pattern book called *Shoppell's Modern Houses* published by architect R.W. Shoppell's New York firm, the Co-operative Building Plan Association. The house was to cost $3,550, and the suggested color scheme in Colonial Revival taste was moss-green-stained roof shingles over silver-gray stained walls, with ivory-white trim. Sometimes referred to as Dutch Colonial style, gambrel-roofed houses like this derive from early Dutch farmhouses in and around New York. The asymmetrical house has a tower-like bay window, whose roof-ridge merges seamlessly into the left gable. Common to Shingle designs, among the Colonial Revival details seen here are the swagged plaster friezes of the bay and dormer, the dormer's small balustrade with finials, the Classical columns of the porch, and the diamond-paned windows. Typical also is the fieldstone used on the foundation and chimneys.

appeared that paved the way for a greater flurry of shingle designs, especially after 1900. Before 1910, some of the best local examples had already been built. The style was also adopted in the East Bay, especially in Berkeley, and it also appeared in Oakland. Bernard Maybeck's steep-roofed shingle house (1895) for Charles Keeler was his first residential commission, and other similar buildings inspired Keeler's book, *The Simple Home* (1904). Both Keeler and Maybeck were involved in the founding of the Hillside Club, a civic-improvement association, which sought to encourage housing designs that blended in with the Berkeley Hills.

Keeler's influential house effectively launched Maybeck into a career of designing innovative houses especially in Berkeley, and in other parts of the Bay Area. He also shone in other projects. In 1898, he was entrusted with handling the new master-plan competition at the University of California at Berkeley, when he established a working relationship with an important supporter of the school, Phoebe Apperson Hearst. Among his many other projects were the brilliant First Church of Christ, Scientist in Berkeley (1910), and the Palace of Fine Arts at the 1915 Panama Pacific Exposition in San Francisco, both of which survive.

Maybeck was probably the most prominent member of a

group of talented and progressive architects working in the Bay Area around the turn of the century. Their domestic designs defined a distinctively local interpretation of the Shingle style and established the region as a center of progressive domestic architecture at an early date. Now identified as an unofficial architectural movement, the period has been described by historians as the "First Bay Area Tradition"; the term is now most commonly used in its shorter version, the "First Bay Tradition."

Most of these architects arrived in the Bay Area in the 1890s, and their houses employed influences that went beyond the Shingle style, including the Swiss Chalet, Craftsman, and Mission Revival styles. Their work was characterized by multi-level floor plans, quirky but often dramatic sequences of spaces, axial relationships, and an unexpected sense of scale and detailing. In addition to Maybeck, the architects usually associated with the "First Bay Tradition" are A. Page Brown, Ernest Coxhead, John Galen Howard, Louis C. Mullgardt, Willis Polk, and A.C. Schweinfurth. The early work of these architects continued to inspire their successors; a "Second Bay Tradition" emerged in the 1930s and 1940s, and was most notably represented by William Wurster.

150. Shingle-style house, San Francisco (1892). The design of this house suggests that its architect, Samuel Newsom, was familiar with East Coast Shingle houses that had been widely promoted by then. Newsom, a prolific local architect, is best known for Queen Anne designs. The successive overhangs of the gables are a way of borrowing extra space beyond the foundation line of the tight lot. Such overhangs of second floors are seen in seventeenth-century homes in New England, and they, in turn, derive from medieval houses. The structural beams and brackets beneath the overhangs anticipate the Craftsman style. The porch area is skillfully designed for access from the steep street, and it contains a large rounded and windowed form beneath the overhang. The unusual hoods on the upper gable and dormer windows are well integrated into the roof. The flared-out walls of the second floor shed water away from the house. Situated in the Presidio Heights area, the house adjoins a famous enclave of exceptional Bay Area Shingle-style houses that are near a gateway to the Presidio. The house backs up to a wooded area that was recently converted from a military base to a national park.

151. Shingle-style houses, San Francisco (1909). Spilling down a Presidio Heights hillside, here are two distinctive and mutually sympathetic houses close to the Presidio gate. Designed by legendary Bay Area architect Bernard Maybeck for Samuel Goslinsky, the house at the left well represents his whimsical yet practical imagination. On a typical twenty-five-foot-wide city lot, the stepped-back design recesses the three-storey, hipped-roof main structure off the street. Set behind a single storey section, the roof line of which parallels the slope of the street, the main part of the house gains extra light. Among the unusual features are the oversized, unmatched cornices, the opposing angles of two curving fascia boards over windows of different heights and sizes, the small tower-like form at the left, and a Classical pediment above the glass-paneled front doors. The other house at the right, designed by William Knowles, was built shortly after the first owner purchased the lot in 1908. In the high-pitched gable, a Gothic-arch window is set into the projecting front—a surprising variation of the Palladian-window design, which is repeated on the side. Arching courses of shingles emphasize the pointed arch. This hillside design has the garage on the lowest level at the right, and above it a shed-roofed section abuts the high gable and mirrors the slope of the hillside. On the uphill side the recessed entry has a turned-spindle screen wall on the left side to admit light.

152. Detail of the Samuel Goslinsky house. On the left side of the house shown in figure 151 is this pair of Gothic-inspired windows on the outside corner of the single-storey section of the house. This playful wooden tracery beautifully mimics stone sculpture on a Gothic cathedral. Between them, the spiraling shape of the copper drainpipe and the bulbous crown of its gutter drain add an exotic element that has been described as "Byzantine."

153. Detail of a Shingle-style house, San Francisco (1902). This is the most remarkable section of a well-known "First Bay Tradition" house designed by noted architect Ernest Coxhead, who had come to the Bay Area from his native England. Situated across the street from the houses in figure 151, this place is part of a noteworthy row of attached Shingle-style houses built "on the wall" of the Presidio, an address much sought after because of its proximity to a peaceful wooded green space in one of San Francisco's finest neighborhoods. In this unusual and striking composition of Georgian-meets-Shingle, simple elements are made dramatic because of exaggerated proportions. Indicated on the exterior by means of a shallow-stepped balcony, an interior staircase ascends between two landings. A visual leveling device, this arrangement offsets the effect of the steep street. The large quasi-Palladian window, set within a recess, reaches nearly to the roof, and only its central section is framed. Set into the shingled façade and defined only by the thinness of their sash, the other windows are plain, uncased rectangles. The front door is compressed beneath an outsized, segmental-arch pediment set on Classical consoles or brackets. The transom and the fanlights framing the door have diamond-pane leaded glass.

154. The Polk-Williams House, San Francisco (1892). Fronting on a steep "stairway street" at the summit of Russian Hill, this intriguing duplex was designed by important local architect Willis Polk, as a double house on a lot sixty feet wide for his family and his client, Mrs. Virgil Williams. Forty feet of the lot were bought by Dora Williams, an artist and the widow of a landscape painter who founded the San Francisco Art Association's School of Design. Although the Polk family lot was only twenty feet wide, their side offered fine views to the east in addition to the sweeping southerly view behind the entire building. At that time Polk's extended family included his wife, his parents, and his grown brother and sister; for several years he worked in partnership with his contractor father and draftsman brother. There was space to accommodate everyone, for rooms stepped down the rear hillside for six storeys; Polk designed his studio to fit on a lower level. While each was completely separate, both houses feature complex vertical floor plans, and extensive redwood paneling. In the asymmetrical shingled façade, Polk expressed the distinct identity of each house; the massing of their projecting upper floors and gables with flaring eaves adapts the forms of urban houses in late medieval France.

155. Shingle-style house, San Rafael, California (1890s). Situated above the older Dominican neighborhood, this house has views of the surrounding hills. While the oversize corner tower recalls those of Queen Anne-style houses, its detailing is entirely of the Shingle style. At its base, a fortress-like battered or flaring wall firmly anchors the house into the hillside. The house is entered through a bold archway set off by the shadows of the recessed porch. Without any ornament, this projecting two-storey porch relies on the boldness of its forms for interest. Behind the low panelized wall a stairway rises to the second-floor porch and leads to the front door on the right side. Opening directly to the entry hall is a so-called split Dutch door, a rather informal feature that also helps ventilation.

157. Parlor in the San Rafael house. Clad in tongue-in-groove redwood paneling on the walls and ceiling like the entry, this room's informality suggests that the house may have been built as a summer residence. Opposite a Renaissance Revival cabinet with a bronze plaque and mirror is the doorway to the entry hall. The sweeping curve of windows is the bay seen in the lower section of windows on the tower exterior. The two windows at the left are the ones covered by the front porch. A built-in windowseat extends the full width of the bay and has a series of hinged seats that lift for storage. The homeowners collect American Victorian furniture and decorative arts of the Aesthetic Movement and Eastlake style; most of the furniture in this room is in the Renaissance Revival style. Manufactured by Jeliff, the high-style parlor set has small bronze cameo plaques set in the crest rail of each chair. The ebonized Aesthetic center table, of unusually complex form, is heavily carved and gilded.

156. *(Opposite)* Entry and staircase of the San Rafael house. Rising behind a handsomely turned post and spindlework screen, the main staircase leads to a landing before turning to complete its ascent to the bedroom floor. The walls and ceiling of this room are paneled in California redwood, with a floor of fir. Next to a Hunzinger side chair, a built-in ledge provides useful display space for an Aesthetic Movement lamp, and equally Aesthetic are the art-glass lantern with Japanesque bird-and-blossom motifs and the Middle Eastern textile on the ebonized Eastlake table below the window. In the oval frame near the table are two of the homeowner's Victorian ancestors.

Hybrid Styles
Singular Combinations of Multiple Styles

Although it is always possible to "read" Victorian houses for clues to their governing style, the results are often debatable and/or inconclusive. It usually becomes apparent that the architecture of many houses has been influenced by more than one style; sometimes several can be found. The challenge is that of evaluating which style dominates the others. This has been the general guide in evaluating the styles of the houses illustrated in the previous chapters of this book.

Just as Victorian houses epitomize an eclectic age, so does reading these houses invariably challenge the eye and mind. The captions that describe the illustrations in the various chapters often mention the influence of several styles. This shows that there are few pure, unadulterated, Victorian houses, because that concept is a contradiction in terms; it is, in essence, missing the point. In some ways this chapter is a catch-all for houses discovered during the preparation of this book that eluded the tag of a dominant style. It is also included to promote the joy of learning to read Victorian houses. Each of us has a threshold of perception that allows some things in and edits others out. Therefore, the houses illustrated in this chapter may well prove to be more challenging to evaluate.

In many ways, these hybrid-style houses are among the most interesting and thought-provoking of all the examples, simply because they are those that are more likely to challenge the eye and mind. The most original houses are often the most complex and illogical ones; these shine on their own as simply having been made to delight and even nurture the eye.

The unselfconscious abandon that seems to hover around Victorian houses can be a true tonic for modern anomie, and even help us to remember what is important in life. Fun, amusement, delight, and whimsy: these are key words and feelings that seem to galvanize most fans of Victorian houses. Few Victorians can be admired for their fusion of architectural and philosophical integrity. Instead, most Victorians are admired for providing a glimpse into another world that is both familiar and comforting, perhaps exotic, and even disarming. Like the complex personalities of people, Victorian houses have never pleased everyone, and they never will. After all, many were derided in their own time as vehemently as they were with the advent of the Modern Movement, when they seemed to be the antithesis of anything sensible or useful, let alone beautiful.

However, those who have come to realize that Victorians are worth getting to know better have learned that these houses have a lot to say to those who are willing to listen. The point is that in the process of listening, valuable things can be learned about old houses. And having listened carefully, more and more of us will eventually come to understand the intrinsic value of respecting our past and continuing to learn from it, rather than dismissing it as having outlived its usefulness.

Fig. 1

Fig. 2

Fig. 3

Fig. 4

Fig. 5

Fig 7

Fig. 8

Fig 6

Scale: ½ inch to the foot.

Sam.ˡ Sloan, Arch.ᵗ

P. S. Duval's Steam Lith. Press Philad.ᵃ

158. Details of an "Oriental villa" (1852). Reproduced from a pattern book called *The Model Architect* by Philadelphia architect Samuel Sloan, this plate shows exterior details of a country house the style of which could be only described as Moorish Revival. Architectural forms derived from Moorish Spain were applied to an otherwise conventional Italianate villa that was rectangular in plan, with two stories, a shallow hipped roof, and a square central tower. Topped by an onion dome, seen at the right, the tower's cornice, brackets, and windows are shown in the center. Described as a minaret, the form at the left ornamented the corners of the roof. A smaller onion dome at the lower left was used for large finials above a two-storey front porch. The cornice and brackets of the main roof are drawn at the lower right; the open circle in the frieze indicated an attic-level window. Several variations of the Moorish horseshoe arch, seen here (at the center) were used above windows and between porch columns; some were the scalloped type shown in figure 159.

159. Vedanta Society's Hindu Temple, San Francisco (1905). Located in the Cow Hollow neighborhood, this building was built as the headquarters of the Vedanta Society of Northern California led by Swami Trigunatitananda, who had founded the group in 1900. He worked with its architect, Joseph A. Leonard, and advised him on doctrinal matters of Hinduism that affected its design. The overall form and features of the first two floors seem typical of corner Edwardian-era buildings; the classical columns flanking the recessed main entry at the left, and the shield-shaped motifs with ribbons ornamenting the façade, bay windows, and cornice suggest the Colonial Revival style. In addition, there are Moorish-style elements, such as the window transoms with multi-lobed arches along the side of the first floor and the onion-dome canopy over a rear entrance. Then there is the extraordinary Arabian nights skyline of a complexity unparalleled in San Francisco that crowns it all. Emphasized by shadows, the third floor has an outside walkway set behind a continuous arcade of multi-lobed horseshoe arches with an outwardly bowed wrought-iron railing between them. Above all this fishscale shingles cover a "French cap" roof that is topped by all manner of towers and domes. The local group that built this was formed as a result of the popularity of the teachings of Swami Vivhananda at Chicago's 1893 World's Columbian Exposition. Through their building's amazing combination of forms, the group was seeking to express a basic Vedanta tenet (the common doctrinal basis of all Hinduism): all religions are paths to one goal.

160. (Opposite) Stick/Eastlake/Queen Anne/Moorish Revival-style flats, San Francisco (1894). Architects Laver & Mullany included various Moorish-inspired elements in this building. Among them are the horseshoe arch on the square tower, the crisscrossing pattern of the frieze and second-floor railing, and the angles in and around the front doors. The Queen Anne style is reflected in the overall composition of the entry portico, the slanted bay windows behind a screen of columns, and in the patterned shingles of the roof-cap cornice and atop the tower. Stick/Eastlake influence is seen in the lines of the cornice brackets that continue down the façade, and in the line of arcading below the first-floor bay window.

161. Octagon House, San Francisco (1861). The shape of this house provides its greatest distinction, and it remains one of two octagonal houses in San Francisco that have survived since the mid-nineteenth century (see fig. 71). In terms of its exterior style, only three of its architectural elements are in the Italianate style: the quoins that delineate the eight shallow corners, the cupola, and the hipped roof. While octagonal houses had very limited popularity, their concept became widely known as the result of a book on the subject by Orson S. Fowler called *A Home for All*, first published in 1848. Fowler was a progressive, reform-minded man who became a phrenologist, but is best known as an amateur architect who believed that an octagonal house conserved space, saved building materials, created efficient floor plans, and helped create a more healthful physical and mental environment. Most octagonals had a central stairway lit by the cupola, which also helped air circulation. Even Fowler's suggested building material was innovative; he recommended a concrete-like mixture, which he called "grout," or "gravel wall" made of simple natural materials: coarse sand, gravel, and lime. This was cast into a shell of sturdy and economical walls to which different exterior claddings could be applied. Acquired in 1953 by the National Society of The Colonial Dames of America in California, the house was moved to its present location and remodeled for use as their state headquarters. It is also a museum of decorative arts and historic documents of the Colonial and Federal periods. On display is a time capsule prepared in 1861 by the first owners that contains newspapers, a family photo, and is addressed to "Future Ages."

162. Italianate/Stick/Eastlake-style flats, San Francisco (c.1880s). There are elements in this façade that suggest the Italianate style, but each has been restyled to appear more in the Stick/Eastlake taste. The parts derived from the Italianate style include the corner quoins at the first floor, a columned portico and balustraded balcony with large finials, a pedimented window cap, and colonnettes flanking all the windows. Sprigs of wooden laurel leaves above the windows add a formal touch more consistent with the Italianate style. Entirely typical Stick/Eastlake elements are the squared bay, the cornice brackets that connect to other façade elements, and the geometric flat-sawn ornament and patterning, especially in the cornice and below each bay window.

163. Italianate/Second Empire/Classical Revival/Queen Anne-style house, San Francisco (c.1890s). Anchoring a corner of the Hayes Valley neighborhood, this building is composed mostly in the Italianate and Second Empire styles. Not typical of either of these is the Queen Anne corner tower, and the lavish use of oversize Classical columns suggests the Classical Revival style. The strong horizontals of the floor levels are offset by the verticality of the columns, which are taller on the second floor, and which emphasize the tower and squared bay. Pedimented window caps in the Italianate taste occur on the dormers between the bays and in the rear section with the glassed-in rooftop porch. Also typical of that style are the segmental arch-topped windows used in both bays. More obscured here by other elements than in most examples of its style is the curving Second Empire-style mansard roof.

164. Stick/Eastlake/Queen Anne-style flats, San Francisco (1897). The linking of the cornice brackets to elements of the façade is a usual Stick device, and the incised brackets, plain panelized cornice, and flat-sawn ornament indicate an Eastlake influence. Above the square bay that is also associated with these styles is a cut-out notch in the cornice that provides additional interest. These elements are used in combination with several Queen Anne-style details, including the arched front portico with bulbous turned posts and ball-and-stick spindlework, the fishscale shingles on the upper section of the second floor, and the ornate carvings used on the lower bay and above the single window at the right. This building may have been built as a single-family dwelling and later converted into two flats, a common fate of many San Francisco Victorian houses.

165. Queen Anne/Colonial Revival-style house, San Francisco (c.1895). The overall proportions and massing of this imposing Pacific Heights house are Queen Anne style, while most of the details are in Colonial Revival taste. The fishscale shingling of the French-cap roof above the second-floor bay at the right is a simplified version of a typical Queen Anne feature with roots in the Second Empire. The pair of arched windows above the main entrance is Italianate in form, but its art-glass panels are typically Queen Anne. Also filled with art glass is the oval window next to it and the circular one in the attic gable incorporating the initial C, shapes that are generally associated with the Colonial Revival. That style is also reflected in the narrow wood siding, the Classical columns, and the panelized frieze of the Queen Anne tower. The small third-floor windows were probably for servants' quarters.

166. Queen Anne/Colonial Revival house, San Francisco (c.1895). The elaborate carving in the gable peak and in the second-floor panels suggests the carved masonry of the Romanesque Revival. The symmetrical composition of the second floor is defined by unusual curved-glass windows at each outside corner that echo the rounded stucco of the large attic opening. The relationship of the portico to the slanted bay at the left is typical of Queen Anne houses. Of modified Classical proportions, the first floor's frieze, columns, and railing suggest the Colonial Revival and anticipate the Edwardian era.

167. McConaghy House, Hayward, California (1886). Once part of an extensive country estate, this house survives as a link to this city's once-rural past. The house combines elements of both the Stick/Eastlake and Queen Anne styles. The Stick style is seen in the use of squared bay windows; the placement of the cornice brackets reflects that style's practice of aligning them with windows and other structural elements. Simple geometric detailing and milled ornament in the gable peaks and above windows, and the turned spindlework spandrels across the top of the porch between posts are in the Eastlake taste. The top of each window is outlined with a stylized version of a Gothic Revival "drip" molding. Extensive iron cresting adds a stylish, vaguely Gothic flourish above the length of the porch and on top of the hipped roof. The Queen Anne influence is chiefly found in the wrap-around front porch, perhaps the most distinguished feature of the house. Also Queen Anne is the overall asymmetrical massing and the pedimented tops of the bays piercing the hipped roof. Furnished in period style as a house museum, the McConaghy House and grounds are open to the public.

(Overleaf) 168. Winchester House, San Jose, California (c.1884–1922). One of the most extraordinary and puzzling Victorian structures in America, this house was the obsession of Mrs. Sarah L. Winchester, who was the widowed heiress to the Winchester Rifle fortune. Sarah was born into a prominent New Haven, Connecticut, family and married William Wirt Winchester in 1862. Because of the death of their infant daughter in 1866, she sank into a deep depression that was compounded by her husband's death of tuberculosis in 1881. She sought the advice of a Boston spiritualist, who supposedly gave her the motivation to construct the house. It is said that the medium told Sarah that her family and its fortune was haunted by the spirits of all the thousands of restless dead who had been killed by Winchester rifles, and that her own daughter and husband had been their untimely victims. Sarah was instructed to move West; there she could appease the spirits by building them a large house. As long as its construction continued, Sarah's life would not be in danger, and she would also gain eternal life. So she went to California, and after visiting a niece who lived in nearby Menlo Park, she found and purchased this property in 1884, which was then an unfinished eight-room farmhouse that was absorbed by the present structure. Sarah eventually acquired a total of 161 acres of prime agricultural land surrounding the house and operated a successful fruit-farming business. But the building of the house never stopped until the day she died in 1922. By that time, she had spent an estimated $5,500,000 on the house that, still unfinished, contained 160 rooms. The house contains two thousand doors, ten thousand windows, forty-seven stairways, forty-seven fireplaces, thirteen bathrooms, and six kitchens. The architecture is chiefly Queen Anne, but combined with Stick, Eastlake, Shingle, and Colonial Revival styles. Before extensive damage caused by the same 1906 earthquake that hit San Francisco, there was a tall section including a seven-storey tower that rose from the center of this view. Placed on the National Register of Historic Places in 1974, it is California Registered Historic Landmark #868. Most widely known as the Winchester Mystery House, both the residence and gardens are open to the public.

169. Detail of the façade of Winchester House. Hinting at the layers of complexity in this structure that ceaselessly evolved over thirty-eight years, this view is a detail of part of the house in the middle of the view in figure 168. Some parts of the building are more artistically successful than others; however, when they are considered individually, many of the details are conceived with charming and original effect, such as the inverted teardrop-shape, shingle-covered underside of the tower at the right, and the tiny circular open balcony above. A trio of front-parlor art-glass windows are at the lower right.

170. Detail of the Central Garden at Winchester House. Part of the beautifully landscaped grounds, this area has the enclosed feeling of a courtyard and was overlooked by Mrs. Winchester's bedroom at the left. The windowless tower is actually an elevator shaft. Below the tower to the right is an aviary; the windows that wrap around the corner admit daylight to the South Conservatory. Out of view is a crescent-shaped flower bed within a boxwood hedge, which supposedly had occult meaning for Mrs. Winchester.

171. Detail of the greenhouse at Winchester House. In order to blend with the house at the right, this unusual structure has glass-paned dormers and cupolas that were set into solid roofs above the trellised arches. This greenhouse ensured a continuous supply of flowering potted plants to be used inside the house throughout the year.

172. *(Opposite)* Detail of the front façade of Winchester House. Vivid roses emblazon the front garden that frames the house. The front door is aligned with the white-trimmed peak of the portico behind the juniper. The central gable is elegantly shingled, and the turned ball-and-stick railing of the recessed balcony is typically Queen Anne; a pair of circular flower-like carvings and other panelized wall areas of the first floor suggest English influence.

173. Grand Ballroom in Winchester House. Costing more than $9,000, when many middle-class houses were being built for less than $1,000, this is the largest and most extravagantly decorated room in the house. However, it seems probable that it was never used as a ballroom. Mrs. Winchester was a trained pianist, and supposedly she was sometimes heard playing the organ in the middle of the night. Designed for the use of musicians, two small recessed alcoves with the tops of the openings decorated with elaborate fretwork spandrels simulating drapery are situated at both the left and right of the fireplace wall. Although the surround is noticeably absent, the Eastlake-inspired design of the fireplace mantel is an integral part of a room-wide arrangement of built-in shelves, most of which are not in place. The art-glass windows contain unfamiliar quotations from Shakespeare that must have had some special significance for Mrs. Winchester. The red and gold wallcovering is not original. The fine woods in this room include mahogany, teak, maple, rosewood, oak, and white ash. The parquet floor has a complex geometric pattern in its inlaid border. The German silver gas chandelier fitted with glass "candles" is original.

174. Front parlor in Winchester House. Overlooking the front garden, this room was the receiving room for visitors. After Mrs. Winchester's death, the contents of the house were auctioned off by her niece, so these and other furnishings including the draperies are not original to the house. Outstanding craftsmanship is seen in the intricately inlaid geometric pattern of the hardwood floor and its surrounding border. The embossed frieze, cornice, and all of the various ceiling elements are made of Lincrusta, a popular and durable embossed wallcovering similar to linoleum. The frieze has a bold pattern of scallop shells; on the ceiling, a series of interlocking rectangles are filled with delicate overall patterning. A large Renaissance Revival-style mirror that predates this house sits above a robustly scaled wooden mantel. The floral motifs of the olive-green tile surround show Aesthetic Movement taste.

175. Detail of the "Twin Dining Rooms" in Winchester House. Found in both dining rooms, this handsome Lincrusta wainscot shows a finishing in which the relief was accented with paint to highlight pattern and texture.

176. Fireplace of the "Twin Dining Rooms" in Winchester House. Set in its own alcove, this fireplace is one of the most striking in the house. The exotic, rather Moorish aspect of its decoration is another example of the Aesthetic Movement influence that Mrs. Winchester must have favored. Spanning the width of the alcove, this mantel has crisply faceted patterning that provides bright accents together with the small panes of beveled glass above the fireplace opening. Japanesque birds and sunrays decorate the bottom of the fireplace. In the corner recesses at the left and right is another embossed Lincrusta pattern of stylized daisies (Mrs. Winchester's favorite flower) in the Aesthetic taste.

177. Master bedroom in Winchester House. Spacious and airy, this room is where Mrs. Winchester died in 1922. An inviting alcove with a piano at the right has a fireplace with a marble surround, a mirror and lights over the mantel, and built-in bookcases at either side. As is the case in the rest of the house, none of these furnishings is original (the impressive Renaissance Revival bed and dresser are of an earlier date), but are an attempt to recreate the feeling of Mrs. Winchester's occupancy; only a few of the rooms are completely furnished. The windows of the bay straight ahead overlook the Central Garden. Remarkably intact, stylish, and repainted, the Lincrusta wallcovering, coved cornice, and paneled ceiling are original.

178. Bedroom fireplace in Winchester House. The presence of whimsy in much of the decoration in this house suggests that Mrs. Winchester must have had a more lighthearted side than her general reputation suggests, and that she also probably derived much genuine enjoyment out of her endless building project. This quasi-Oriental fireplace is located in a small bedroom in an intimate suite close to the master bedroom. The mantel is constructed and ornamented with faux bamboo. In its upper section are cupboard doors with oval panels of "bamboo" fretwork that open to shallow storage space.

The Edwardian Era
Postscript for the Victorian Age

More than a decade before San Francisco's 1906 earthquake and fire, the sense of a new beginning had already pervaded the Bay Area. After Victorian architecture had culminated in the Queen Anne style, local building professionals had begun to gravitate toward Classicism, and its earliest expression was in commercial and public buildings. Public taste was increasingly ready to accept Classical restraint in their new houses, but it took the post-1906 building boom to suppress the local tradition of excess long established by Victorian domestic architecture. The more straightforward quality of the new Edwardian-era housing was a welcome change, and perfectly suited to the City's optimistic mood of renewal.

When the 1906 disaster occurred, the Edwardian age (1901–1914) was half over, but those buildings that now define the period in San Francisco were about to proliferate more quickly, and in greater quantities, than those of any previous period or style. For this reason, the Edwardian era is one of the most significant in San Francisco's history; yet its surviving residential buildings are often dismissed as being less interesting or significant than the Victorians. However, the Edwardian buildings of San Francisco define the brilliant period of its reconstruction, which earned the City worldwide respect and admiration.

The neighborhoods that are almost entirely comprised of Edwardian-era buildings are fascinating to observe and study. What prevails among them is a quality of restraint that seems plain in comparison to most Victorian houses. Their ornament tends to be limited, and is almost invariably derived from a classical vocabulary. The examples selected for this chapter all show this influence, apparent in their entry portico columns, bracketed cornices, and assorted moldings with Classical profiles: dentil and egg-and-dart moldings were among the most popular. For mostly economic reasons the ceilings of Edwardian buildings are lower, and their windows are there-

fore shorter than typical Victorian examples, which were derided as being wasteful. Edwardian roofs are often flat; most designs also tend to have a greater horizontal emphasis.

The 1906 San Francisco earthquake and fire not only wiped out all of the downtown shopping and financial districts but also the adjoining older neighborhoods of Nob Hill, Russian Hill, North Beach and Telegraph Hill, and South of Market; significant parts of the Mission District and Hayes Valley were also destroyed. Therefore these are the areas in which to find the City's best Edwardian-era buildings. They create a remarkably cohesive streetscape that is most apparent in the residential side streets of the rebuilt neighborhoods.

When the destroyed neighborhoods were rebuilt, they typically became much more crowded. Far fewer single-family houses were rebuilt and still remain rare in these neighborhoods. Some of the most popular multi-unit buildings were the two- or three-flat variety. Often owner-occupied, these allowed the option of housing extended families in conveniently close but separate quarters, or provided extra rental income for the owner. Kept full by the steady stream of new arrivals were larger apartment buildings and residential hotels that tended to offer lower rents. While they occurred in other areas, they proliferated near downtown, especially on the lower slopes of Nob Hill, across the "Tenderloin," and into the South of Market and Mission districts. Many of these buildings were constructed with steel frames or reinforced concrete, but some unreinforced-masonry buildings were also rebuilt, and these remain the most seismically problematic today. Outside of the downtown apartment buildings, almost everything else was rebuilt of wood, but without the requisite "fretsawn furbelows" of the Victorian structures.

The speed with which the destroyed parts of San Francisco were rebuilt was truly breathtaking. Its progress was highly touted by local boosters and well documented in

179. Edwardian-era mixed-use building, San Francisco (c.1905). On a shopping street with other mixed-use buildings that combine residential and commercial spaces, this structure has retained the original plan of its first-floor space, which was designed for up to three offices. This area is fitted with so-called Chicago windows—large fixed central panels set between two smaller operable ones—that were often used on that city's progressive commercial architecture. Typical of local Edwardian-era buildings is the spare use of ornament, the smooth walls made with tightly fitted horizontal wood siding, the combination of angled and bow-front bay windows, and the gracefully rounded bay that anchors the corner. Classical influences are quoins framing the entrances, colonnettes, curving brackets or consoles above the third-floor windows, and the egg-and-dart molding at the cornice line beneath the squared brackets.

180. Edwardian-era flats, San Francisco (c.1905). Rounded bow-front bay windows and a semicircular portico add movement to the façade of these flats in the Haight-Ashbury district. Although the neighborhood has mostly Queen Anne-style buildings, there are many Edwardian examples, especially on the fringes. This overall form is Classically inspired, and some of the repeating motifs in its cast-plaster friezes are similar to those found on Colonial Revival buildings. Above a plain cornice a curved railing with turned balusters encloses a balcony. The large dormer has Classical fluted pilasters and capitals, and both dormers have hipped roofs that spring from the main roof. A marbleized finish was recently applied within the narrow vertical panels that accent the façade.

photographs. The construction of new housing was still a money-making venture, but the urgent necessity of rebuilding housing for the thousands who had lost their homes in 1906 also made it a pressing civic duty. Not only was there great pressure from the public, but the City also did everything it could to encourage the overworked developers and builders to produce new housing as quickly as possible. For example, significant tax incentives were offered to those who could complete new housing within the year of 1907; this resulted in a high number of existing Edwardian buildings in San Francisco that date to that year.

Soon after, the City committed itself to hosting the 1915 Panama-Pacific Exposition, as much to celebrate and show off its reconstruction as to commemorate the opening of the Panama Canal. Moreover, the several years of advance notice for this event was an added reason for the City to push for new construction and civic improvements of all kinds, for all the world would soon be watching the Bay Area.

By all accounts, the event was a stunning success. The triumphant 1915 Exposition injected new pride and muscle into the culture and economy of the San Francisco Bay Area, thus helping to establish the vibrant business of tourism that persisted long after the fair, and which was to become the most important local industry of all.

181. Detail of the portico of the Edwardian-era flats. In this photograph we can see the elegance of the cast-plaster frieze of the portico. The curving lines of the cornice above are emphasized by the dentil molding. Accented with gold leaf, the carved capitals of the paired fluted columns are not of any antique order, but their design of stylized acanthus leaves appears to have been inspired by the Romanesque style.

182. Edwardian-era hotel, San Francisco (1904). First constructed as the Jefferson Hotel and now called the Red Victorian, it is located on a major commercial stretch of Haight Street just east of Golden Gate Park. In continuous use since it was built, it has been operated as a bed-and-breakfast inn since 1978 by its present owner. Typical of many local Edwardian-era buildings is the simple detailing that includes the egg-and-dart and dentil moldings used below the cornice, which is supported by curved Classical brackets of cast plaster. Recently added by the owner, the sunburst ornaments on the bay windows refer to the famous psychedelic heyday of this neighborhood during the late 1960s. A magnet for legions of hippies and flower children, the area's attraction peaked in 1967 during the so-called Summer of Love. The area continues to attract the nostalgic and curious from around the world, and the owner considers this hotel to be the spiritual center of the Haight/Ashbury, intended to commemorate the most positive aspects of the area's colorful past, as well as the various progressive movements (i.e. peace, ecology, and human potential) that grew in its wake.

183. Edwardian-era apartments, San Francisco (c.1910). At the foot of a steep block leading to the top of Nob Hill (note the steps next to the sidewalk at the right), this corner building is similar to many that were quickly rebuilt here and in other nearby neighborhoods (Russian Hill, North Beach, and South of Market) close to the downtown area that were destroyed by the 1906 earthquake and fire. Now dwarfed by the white looming mass of the Masonic Auditorium, this building is in nearly original condition. It is presently operated as a hotel called The Nob Hill Inn. The walls have the fine horizontal texture of narrow wooden siding. On the right side, original art-glass windows bring light and air to the main staircase. Most multiple-unit dwellings like this usually had rather small rooms, and the many bay windows, especially the large rounded-corner variety, added light, views, and usable space.

184. Edwardian-era flats, San Francisco (c.1905). Beneath a cornice of Classical brackets and moldings, an otherwise plain frieze retains some cast-plaster swags and ribbons, which must have originally appeared above each bay window. Other Classically derived elements are the colonnettes at the windows, the pilasters at the open stairway, and the railings with turned balusters. The ground floor's cast-concrete facing simulates quarried-stone blocks. Located in the Western Addition near Alamo Square, this building is larger than it appears, for it continues toward the right to include another covered staircase and more bay windows. Named for their balcony-like stair landings, such buildings are sometimes locally called "Romeo" flats.

185. *(Opposite)* Edwardian-era house, San Francisco (1912). At first glance, the mansard roof of this elegantly massive Presidio Heights house suggests that it might be an example of the Second Empire style. However, this neighborhood was mostly developed after 1900, long after that style had fallen from fashion. Designed by architect Oliver Everett in what might be called French Revival style, the house was built for John Andrew Bergerot, a prominent citizen in San Francisco's French community. It is interesting to note that the brackets under the second-storey windows are superimposed over the capitals of the pilasters beneath them. Colonial Revival forms are the Palladian window in the dormer and the broken pediment and finial below the dormer. A Baroque feature are the volutes, the coiled forms that flank the dormer and the second-storey windows.

186. Detail from the Edwardian-era house. This handsome carved detail that appears at one side of the front door shows the refinement and crisply executed technique that typifies this house. The architect's design skill in the creation of these elements shows his thorough knowledge of Beaux Arts style, which was then at its fashionable peak in upscale residential and public architecture in America. Gold leaf discreetly accents the beauty of the carving.

187. Edwardian-era row house, San Francisco (1910). This house has a stately presence and includes elements of both Classical and Colonial Revival styles. It is a rare single-family house in a part of the Mission District that burned in 1906 and was mostly rebuilt with multi-unit dwellings. With a balustrade across its width, a flat roof forms an open roof deck in front of a set-back top floor. Offset to the left by a long flight of stairs, an imposing portico with a bow-front balcony has fluted Ionic columns that are matched by the pilasters framing the bay window. The graceful broken pediment above the entry has a pair of wreaths highlighted in gold leaf, and the frieze with a cornice of small curved brackets and dentil molding connects the portico to the bay window. A similar frieze and cornice decorate the area under the balustrade.

Before and After

Transformations of Restoration and Renovation

Buildings and houses define much of our collective cultural past. Their state of preservation says much about our respect for that past and should point us toward future priorities.

The examples illustrated in this chapter present a clear message that old houses *are* worth all the trouble involved in making a caring restoration. Benefits extend beyond that of simply improving one's personal environment. Because they can be shared with the world, these projects might be considered outright gifts to their communities. The presence of beautiful buildings serves to enhance the daily lives of all who pass by and through them.

The argument that taking good care of our historic architecture makes economic sense is compelling when a city like San Francisco is used as the example. Blessed with a wealth of domestic architecture that is inextricably linked to its appeal as a tourist destination, there is no doubt that it is in the City's best interest to nurture and care for its old houses. But even in San Francisco, it is not just the prospect of the pleasure given to tourists that motivates their preservation. These are people's homes that are lived in and loved for all sorts of individual reasons. When a vital balance is struck between the private reasons for investing in old houses and the benefit for a community, everyone comes out ahead.

The potential difficulties in restoring and maintaining old houses deters many people from considering becoming involved with them. Many dismiss the prospect for reasons of time and/or money, but fortunately there seems to be a reasonably steady supply of old-house devotees, and historic buildings continue to change hands. There is not always a rational reason to invest in an old building, but doing so can offer a reward that goes far beyond the need for shelter or for the less tangible issues of fashion and status.

There is no simple answer to the question of what is the right way to deal with the repair and maintenance of vintage buildings. Is meticulous restoration better than sensitive renovation? Who decides what approach is the most appropriate? The more easily defined approach is that of restoration, for the design, material, and construction options tend to be very specific: as much as is humanly possible, one should put back "as it was" what was once there. Many people who have significant historic houses consider themselves only temporary stewards and are idealistic in their determination to preserve something from our past.

Not everyone shares this ideal; many refuse to be restricted by what they should or shouldn't do to their house. For them, therefore, the route to fixing up the house will most likely be renovation. This approach has fewer rules of procedure. Unless a property has landmark status or is in a designated historic district, there are no restrictions on what can or cannot be done to it, other than those related to current building codes (or sometimes the whims of local building inspectors). Furthermore, restrictive covenants that do exist in certain historic neighborhoods are typically just concerned with exteriors and do not protect interiors at all.

Thus there is no best answer to the question of restoration versus renovation, for the circumstances of each case will vary. Personal goals will be a factor, with issues of use, timing, and plans for the future to be considered. The effect on the community needs to be evaluated (i.e., will there be controversy or opposition generated by the project?). Lastly, economics will surely play a significant part.

The best aids with which to traverse the peaks and pitfalls of the old-house world are education and experience (not necessarily in that order). Seeking professional advice is always recommended, yet most of us can gain sufficient education and experience to make good decisions for ourselves by taking the time to be observant, and especially to learn by mistakes (whether one's own or those of others).

Besides its obvious intention to promote, encourage, and perhaps inspire the loving care of old buildings, this chapter also commemorates the extraordinary talents of all the people responsible for these transformations. It bodes well for the future that the ranks of old-house architects, designers and craftspeople are growing, but the most credit must be extended to the homeowners themselves, for their vision and commitment have made possible the preservation of these Victorian treasures.

188. **Before:** Italianate/Stick-style row houses, San Francisco (1884). Although a neighborhood eyesore, this row fared better than other Western Addition Victorians, for many were destroyed (mostly in the 1960s) in the wake of a massive redevelopment scheme. These houses had been allowed to degenerate into varying states of disrepair, and some had lost most of the original detailing that had once unified the row. Designed by architect John P. Gaynor as a real-estate investment for prominent local banker William Sharon, the dwellings were collectively built for $30,000. At the far left is a single matching row house that ends the sequence of three "duplex" row houses divided by their entry stairs and porticoes.

189. **After:** Italianate/Stick-style row houses. Now a cynosure of the neighborhood, the series of façades has been carefully restored to original condition. Because the houses had common features, enough original detailing had survived between them to eliminate guesswork in replicating the many parts required. Each pair of mirror-image row houses has been further unified by a common paint scheme, reinforcing the impression (intended by their design) that they are three larger buildings. Extending into its block from the corner at the right, the row is now part of the Alamo Square Historic District.

190. **Before:** Row house, San Francisco (1872). Like other Victorian houses, this Mission District house was treated to a "would-be Spanish" makeover. The original wood siding was fully slathered with stucco, and a front overhang was topped with terra-cotta roof tiles. The size and shape of its window openings remained intact together with the basic form of a high cornice that incorporated third-floor windows. Other than its scale, little else suggested that it had once been an imposing house surrounded by open land, where its original owner, John English, had raised champion race horses. Known as "The Potato King" because of his vast holdings in potato commodities, English was also a San Francisco City Commissioner. This commodious building of twenty-seven rooms was designed by architect Charles I. Havens for Mr. and Mrs. English and their seven children.

191. **After:** Italianate-style row house. Once again an elegant presence on the block, the house was essentially reborn after its extensive restoration, during which the missing pieces of its façade were painstakingly recreated. Once the exterior coat of stucco was removed, numerous telltale "scars" created a basic road map for what needed to be done. While accurate silhouettes were provided by the outlines of missing millwork, the final form of the more complex elements required educated guesswork and were modeled after similar Italianate houses of comparable scale and quality. Windows set between especially tall brackets distinguish the unusual third-floor cornice. Rich detail enhances the new entry portico and bay-window colonnettes. This house is now a bed-and-breakfast called "The Inn San Francisco."

192. ***Before:*** Italianate-style cottage, San Francisco (c.1880). Most of the original elements, including its well-detailed arched windows, were intact on this modest house near Duboce Park, but its street presence was lackluster. By the time this photo was taken, some renovation (including the addition of a garage in the basement level) had already occurred. Although a tight fit, the garage and driveway were made possible both by the setback of the house and sufficient width of the lot.

193. ***After:*** Italianate-style cottage. An understated makeover, mostly consisting of a carefully considered new paint scheme that employs a restrained use of color and accenting with gold leaf, allows this little house to make a bigger impression. Unusual carved decorations now appear above the front door and windows. Seen in this view (and most likely an early twentieth-century addition) is the curving center parapet above the bracketed cornice. Substantial turned balusters on the restored stair railings add character to the entry. A low iron fence steps up the hillside and encloses a small planted area that helps to offset the severity of the pavement.

194. **Before:** Double parlor of the Brune-Reutlinger House, San Francisco (1886). With the distinct advantage of beginning with "good bones," this room's two distinct parts are divided by an original archway supported by a pair of Corinthian columns. At the far end of the room, an angled bay window faces the street. Another of the room's refined architectural details is a Classical pediment above an open double door at the far left that leads to the entry hall. After paint scrapings were taken and analyzed, it was found that this room was originally painted a soft green with traces of gold leaf—thus the palette used for the renovation.

196. *(Opposite)* **After:** Double parlor of the Brune-Reutlinger House. The architectural motifs used on the Renaissance Revival furniture guided the choice of handprinted wall and ceiling papers with related Classical motifs. On the ceiling and in the perimeter cove, the paper patterns mimic various handpainted and stenciled effects typical of 1880s high-style period interiors. The decorative corner "fans" have a trompe-l'oeil effect that resembles gathered fabric. Stenciling was used on the laurel-leaf border decoration on the underside of the arch and on the door panels at the left. Period-appropriate lighting is ensured by a splendid matching pair of antique gasoliers. The detailing of the gilded Renaissance Revival mirror with the Egyptian head at the left matches the antique valance at the right. Their details were adapted on a new valance made to fit the front angled bay.

195. **After:** Detail of the double parlor of the Brune-Reutlinger House. Emphasized by light on its curving surface, a delicate stencil-like wallpaper pattern based on the Greek anthemion motif appears in the coved plaster cornice and is reversed in the frieze. The picture molding combines gold and silver leaf. The wallpaper design was copied from antique damask. The mixture of several soft colors found in the papers was applied to the ceiling rosettes, the Corinthian capitals on the columns, and to the plaster-relief panels of the archway. Repeated from the frieze, a narrow stencil-like wallpaper border was applied to the bases of the capitals above the faux-marbre finish on the fluting of the columns. A Classical laurel-leaf design stenciled in gold leaf decorates the arch.

197. **Before:** Row house, San Francisco (c.1885). Original wood siding is visible on the side of this Pacific Heights house, the façade of which was obscured beneath a coat of stucco. The shed-roofed entry portico probably dates to the time of its remodel. While lacking original decoration, the window openings and cornice retained their earlier proportions. Decorative millwork on Victorian row houses enhanced their verticality and encouraged the eye to pause at various strategic places. This example shows how their removal throws the whole form off balance.

198. **After:** Italianate/Stick-style row house. A small part of the cornice decoration that survived beneath the stucco was salvaged to help reconstruct this façade; all the other elements had to be recreated. Based on the building's overall form and what traces remained of its original millwork elements, it was determined that this house was originally a hybrid variation of the so-called "San Francisco Stick" style. At the owner's request, the new façade was designed to include more Italianate-style elements; these show mostly in the Classical forms adapted for the stair railing and entry portico, and also in the balcony railing and single window cap.

199. **Before:** Eastlake-style cottage, San Francisco (1886). Overlooking Eureka Valley (or the Castro District) from the back, the house fronts on a street that was regraded in 1912 to a higher level, especially along the downhill side, which changed the entry to this building. Access to the front door became possible only by a bridge-like walkway that was raised above the front yard. More for safety than privacy, the wooden fence is on top of a storey-high retaining wall, with the entry gate on the left side.

200. **After:** Eastlake-style cottage. Without altering its modest character, the Eastlake identity of the house has been significantly increased. The new design is more boldly expressive of the style, yet is historically plausible. Removal of asphalt shingles exposed the original clapboards. The triangular motifs added to the cornice help to activate the gable's blank space, and they also relate to the triangle forms on the front fence. A new entry portico and matching window hoods have incised linear decoration on their pediments, and strengthen the overall design by repeating the roof's angle. Although not original to this house, their form was adapted from a nearby house of similar period and style. The reconstructed front walkway "bridge" traverses the sunken front yard, which is an ideal spot for the rhododendron garden. A definitively Eastlake character is established in the front fence by simple geometric motifs, and the fan shapes ease the level transitions. The use of plain flat boards shaped like balusters, with cutouts that create repeating patterns of positive and negative spaces, was inspired by similarly detailed railings of Swiss chalets.

201. **Before:** Stick-and Italianate-style row houses, San Francisco (c.1880s). This remarkable early view shows these Pacific Heights houses sometime before 1886. The house on the right with two small children visible near the bottom of the front steps was designed by prominent local architects Kenitzer & Raun for Frederick and Anita Weiland, who had paid $6,000 for the lot; the house cost over $10,000 when it was built in 1882. Remaining in the Weiland family until 1993, it was purchased by the current owners, who began restoration in 1994. The house at left dates to 1883, and is believed to have been built for a Judge Morrison, who supposedly used its attic for his large library. In the lumber-rich early years of the City's settlement, it was common practice to use wooden planks (visible here) in lieu of paving for sidewalks. The hillside site required significant grading and the construction of retaining walls in order to be buildable. Seen in the background are Italianate-style houses fronting on the opposite side of the block. The tracks in the middle of the street are those of the California Street cable-car line whose original route extended past these houses.

202. **Before:** Stick- and Italianate-style row houses. The house to the right, built for John Weiland in 1886, was also designed by Kenitzer & Raun. Three garages across the front of the center house were added in the 1920s. The house on the left appears almost unchanged, although its entry steps have been altered, and the attic dormer windows have been changed to a single large opening.

203. **After:** Detail of the Stick- and Italianate-style row houses. The fine craftsmanship of the elegantly reconstructed portico and front steps of the center house is shown here. Also visible are the front doors that have been painted to resemble walnut with inset burled panels.

204. **After:** Detail of the Italianate-style row house. Above the first-floor bay window, a finely modeled head of a Victorian lady has been restored in a prominent position. This view shows how the tasteful arranging of details on the façade creates a unified composition. A subtle paint scheme discreetly employs gold leaf to emphasize the jewel-like quality of smaller elements.

166

205. **After:** Stick- and Italianate-style row houses. This trio of stately houses creates a stunning row on a street already noted for many significant houses. The transformation of the house at center to nearly original condition is complete. One significant change is the development of its attic level into a full floor of living space by the addition of dormer windows set into a shallow mansard roof.

206. **Before:** Edwardian/Colonial Revival-style row house, San Francisco (1896). This home, unusually elegant for its Noe Valley neighborhood, had survived with all of its Classical detailing. Essentially, its makeover was to be just a new paint scheme. In this view, trees obscure the ornate first floor, but it shows how the recessed panels of the frieze beneath a bracketed cornice are carefully aligned with the window widths of the second floor.

207. **After:** Edwardian/Colonial Revival-style row house. A striking color scheme created by one of the owners (an art conservator) has brought the Classical detailing of this house into new prominence. Its transitional character is a combination of the tailored effect typical of the Edwardian era and decorative detailing inspired by the Colonial Revival. Beneath a narrow egg-and-dart molding, motifs of ribbons and wreaths are rendered in cast plaster on the first-floor frieze. Separating the arched windows of the bay and also used at the entry portico are unusual pilasters with simple Ionic capitals on their lower portions and beribboned torches on their faces. A large urn and turned-baluster railings are Classical elements used in the balcony above the portico. In an annual nationwide trade competition, this project won a first-place award for its painting contractor, Local Color, as the "1994 Best Painted House in America."

208. **_Before:_** Queen Anne-style house, San Francisco (c.1895). All of the original decorative millwork of this Ashbury Heights house had been stripped away, and a layer of asbestos shingles was added. Having suffered these indignities, the house still had the advantage of a good location, which encouraged the restoration. The house began life as a Queen Anne cottage, which survives in the part with the forward-facing gable. A taller rear addition with a hipped roof was constructed around 1910.

209. **_After:_** Queen Anne-style house. Now barely discernible as the same building, a sweeping transformation has occurred; its inventive new design could well have occurred in the Queen Anne period. Although no tower previously existed, it was introduced as an effective way to bridge the building's two disparate parts. Added at the old corner location of a single second-floor window, the octagonal tower creates a corner bay. Its graceful bell-shaped roof, covered with fishscale shingles, has a glass-sided lantern incorporated into the base of the tall finial. A new arched gable window repeats the arch of the bay below and the arches in the tower and the recessed entry. The fan shapes and cut-out bargeboard trim are Eastlake details. Another example of hybrid influence is the wooden fence that was adapted from an Italianate-style railing.

210. *Before:* Stick/Eastlake-style house, Santa Rosa, California (c.1885). Surrounded by a lush garden, this house has a generous front porch, and it has retained almost all of its distinctive original detailing. Stick-style elements are on each level of the squared bay at the right. The flat, geometric designs of the cut-out spandrels between the turned porch posts and on the bargeboard trim are Eastlake style. Most of these elements were made nearly invisible in this bland paint scheme, which had attempted to accent the delicate cut-out frieze decoration.

211. *After:* Stick/Eastlake-style house. The goal being to highlight the architectural elements of this house, the paint scheme strikes a good balance with this reliable formula: the darkest value is reserved for the window sash, or as a framing device elsewhere, the medium value provides sufficient weight for the body of the house, and the advancing character of the lightest value brings out the most interesting details. Another medium-dark secondary value gives increased prominence to the frieze and various upper gable areas.

212. **_Before:_** Queen Anne-style flats, San Francisco (c.1895). Stripped before a stucco coating was applied, this Haight/Ashbury District building lost all of its original millwork detailing in a classic example of misguided "remuddling." Even the small tower on the right side of the roof lost a cone-shape "witch's hat." As with other denuded Victorian row houses, especially in the areas between floors and around the windows, the mostly vertical proportions now seem without purpose. Only the basic window openings and angles of its bays have remained unchanged.

213. **_After:_** Queen Anne-style flats. In a masterful façade restoration, the long-lost glory has been mostly recovered for this building. Only its front steps, railings, and garage are obvious additions. The attic-level tower has regained its importance with the replacement of the missing roof, and its cylindrical form is reflected in the gentle outward curve of the windows at the outside corners below on the first and second floors. With a turned-spindle railing, a small shelf-like balcony is placed in front of the paired gable windows, which are framed by bold swirls of carved millwork. The handsome carved vase of flowers centered on the façade of the second floor fills the once conspicuously blank space within an arching frame.

214. **Before:** Detail of the Queen Anne-style flats. Once the stucco was removed from the house, it was possible to study the phantom "scars" that remained, including this one of the large floral centerpiece and arch that were originally on the second-floor façade. Showing in great detail what was missing, the phantom outlines like this one were an effective blueprint for the recreation. Individual forms were not always entirely described by their outlines, and some decorative work had to be based on similar ornament on neighboring houses.

215. **After:** Detail on the Queen Anne-style flats. Once it was restored, the lively second floor centerpiece instantly became a frequently photographed part of this row of Victorians. In an architectural sense, it is an alternate equivalent of a window element; on some other Queen Anne houses, its position might be that of a recessed balcony. This view also makes clear the high quality of the other restored elements, such as the projecting cornice, the tiny Classical capitals on the fluted pilasters, and the various carved decorations on the friezes above each of the first two floors.

216. **Before:** Queen Anne-style row house, San Francisco (c.1895). Located next door to the house illustrated in figures 212-215, the similarity is obvious. The house had been subdivided into separate apartments, and much work needed to be done to make it a single-family home once again.

217. **After:** Queen Anne-style row house. Lavished with attention and improvements, the house is once again a single-family residence and its owner's pride and joy. The vivid new paint scheme with accents of gold and silver leaf features a marbleized finish on the columns of its entry portico and of the third-floor balcony. Corresponding to the central floral carving on the neighboring house, a large snowflake-shaped centerpiece is the focal point of the second floor. Gilded masks decorate the frieze above the first floor. All of the carvings are now revealed in high relief by their light color or metallic accents against a dark background. Now particularly elegant, the front stairs were recently resurfaced in marble. Their original metal railings have received a decorative painted finish that resembles the greenish-blue color of patinated bronze. Probably added in the 1920s, the garage doors have become a fine addition to the overall decorative composition of the house by means of the bright blue panels outlined in red that are set into the dark blue background of the doors—a palette that is used elsewhere on the façade.

Victorian Revival Interiors
The Future of Nineteenth-Century Design

The awakening of the so-called Victorian Revival in America dates to the late 1960s—the end of a tumultuous decade, when it seemed that just about everything in our culture was being reconsidered, challenged, torn apart, or reinvented. It was then that some people (especially members of the younger generation), who had grown up in the throes of the Modern Movement, began to question its authority and appeal. Modernism had dominated popular taste and culture since the 1930s, and in light of the cyclical swing of opinion that is inevitable between generations, many began to long for a more comfortable aesthetic for living.

Although there must have been many who had fully appreciated the experience of growing up in Victorian houses (or with the era's furnishings), they were still in the minority. In fact, the entire aura of the nineteenth century was simply not fashionable; society was obsessed with the future. The landing of a man on the moon in 1969 was a fitting climax to a decade that saw few limits. However, even then, history had its devotees, and there was a steady increase in those who felt intuitively that the Victorian period was something special.

Tangible evidence of this growing interest was when Victorian furniture and other decorative arts began to get second looks, serious notice, and even significant sales at auction. Before long Victorian decorative arts of the finest quality began to be systematically acquired at bargain prices. Wealthy and fashionable tastemakers began to take notice, and nostalgia was on its way to becoming a household word.

The real blossoming of the Victorian Revival occurred in the 1970s, when not only the decorative arts but also the architecture of the period became popular. The concept of urban pioneers that started in the 1960s took hold in many cities, and it became trendy to buy for next to nothing a run-down Victorian house in a marginal neighborhood. For well-educated middle-class people, who were those most likely to pursue renovating old houses at this early date, little was available to guide them through the process. However, demand was slowly met by supply, and it became evident that it was a good business decision to invest in a field that seemed almost wide open and devoid of serious competition for the foreseeable future.

As Victorian Revival mania spread, so did the available resources. The National Trust for Historic Preservation assumed new importance. Preservation and the informed, sensible approach to old buildings that the word implies became a useful and powerful partner of urban pioneerism. Books and periodicals discussing the restoration of Victorian houses became available. One of the earliest periodicals that catered in earnest to the urban-pioneer set (and anyone else who happened to like old buildings) was the *Old House Journal*. It began in the mid-1970s and continues in publication today.

The concept of making a living by restoring old houses, or providing goods or services for the purpose, seemed to emerge across the country in the late 1970s. This was the time

218. *(Opposite)* Entry hall of an Italianate-style row house, San Francisco (1877). This Mission District house was once divided into two flats, but it is once again a single-family home, and an extensive collection of vintage posters, graphics, and illustrations are now displayed in this hall. Only painted finishes have been used here on the woodwork, walls, and ceiling. The period leather-like wainscot of embossed Lincrusta has a finish of deep reddish-brown. The grain-painted finish on the woodwork and doors matches the walnut with burled panels of the stair's newel post. The motif of tropical foliage in the carpet was reproduced from the original in the former royal palace in Honolulu. Many Italianate houses have a display niche similar to the one set into the curved wall near the turn in the staircase. Note the glass "jewels" set into the unusual period brass gasolier. The predominantly green walls have a painted texture of blended colors that is sometimes called a "Tiffany finish."

219. Detail of the ceiling in the entry hall of the row house. This view is directly above the front door. The main section of the painted ceiling has a special finish that adds texture to the handsome shade of terra-cotta. Adding interest in the corners, Classical motifs of laurel leaves and palmettes are stenciled in a light blue-gray, and all is framed by a Greek-key border.

220. Back parlor of the row house. In order to share the light provided by the front parlor's bay window, the wood panels of the original pocket doors were replaced with etched and wheel-cut glass. Their stylized motifs suggest an Eastlake influence, but also recall the work of Dr. Christopher Dresser, an important progressive nineteenth-century English designer, whose work inspired these striking handprinted wallpapers. Dating to the early 1980s, this room project is a Victorian Revival milestone, for it was the first time that a coordinated roomset of dado, filling, frieze, and ceiling papers was installed by Bradbury & Bradbury Art Wallpapers. Accented with gilding and painting that is also used in the plaster ceiling rosette, the coved plaster cornice has wallpaper borders that are set in and above it. The ceiling paper is printed with a "mica" ink to reflect light. The period "Turkish" chairs have typically gathered and tufted upholstery. The carpet pattern matches that in the entry hall, but the colors are different.

221. Detail of the bay window in the front parlor of the row house. Glorifying the angled bay window facing the street, these draperies were inspired by the lavish fabrics and trims shown in period decorating books and periodicals.

222. Dining room of the row house. Inspired by Aesthetic Movement taste, this room scheme is achieved by combining paint, paper, and découpage. Stenciled in a variation of the so-called cracked-ice pattern, the ceiling is divided by plain borders into quadrants that radiate from a central plaster rosette, which is surrounded by intertwined lines that recall Chinese and Celtic knot patterns. The frieze is created with a series of repeating fretwork panels that enclose either painted patterns or elements découpaged from the wallpaper pattern below. The woodwork in this room has been grain-painted to look like golden oak, and the original wainscot embossed with an Islamic-style pattern has a painted metallic finish of dark blue-green. The Renaissance Revival sideboard is an exuberant mélange of Victorian detail.

223. Double parlor of a Stick-style row house, San Francisco (1887).
This double parlor is divided only by a dropped beam supported on
large ornamental plaster brackets; one is visible at the upper left. To
express each part of the room as a separate area, and to offset any
feeling of excessive length or narrowness, there are two ceiling
arrangements, with one visible here. The Classical motifs of the
papers relate to those of the two-tiered mantel, millwork, and plaster
cornice decoration. The architectural quality of the panelized dado
pattern helps unite the room at the floor level, and makes the room
feel wider. The Classical forms of the console at left and the sofa in
the window are sympathetic companions to related motifs found in
the papers. Opening to the back half of this room is the dining room,
and a double doorway to the entry hall is opposite the fireplace.

224. Front parlor of a Victorian flat, San Francisco (c.1890s). Above
a retail store, this flat is in a mixed-use building typical of many
neighborhoods of the City. The Classical form of the fireplace mantel
inspired the selection of the so-called Neo-Grec wall and ceiling
papers for this room, which were adapted from designs published in
the 1880s by English architects George and Maurice Ashdown
Audsley. The fireplace has a mantel painted in a green faux-marbre
finish to go with the papers and includes a quirky but original tile
surround that helps offset the room's formality. The proportions of this
room were ideal for the three-part wall divisions of dado, filling, and
frieze that were popular at this time. Parts of the wallpaper elements
seen around the bay window and in the coved plaster cornice were
cut apart and moved around to fit specific spatial needs. A ceiling
panel above the bay adapts a motif of Terra—one of the four
elements—originally created for tiles by noted English designer
Walter Crane.

225. Three-room view in the Victorian flat. Revealed through doorway openings, a sequence of spaces shows how using different colors and patterns in adjoining rooms can create the effect of a harmoniously complex tapestry. Open to the kitchen, the color scheme of the breakfast room in the foreground is a combination of mossy greens, deep reds, and metallic gold. Its various patterns include a ceiling paper designed by William Morris, and a charming frieze adapted from a Walter Crane design. In lieu of millwork, a stencil-like border trims out the underside of the arch. Next come the kitchen's cool colors in papers that adapt various period designs by Dr. Christopher Dresser. To conceal a refrigerator at the left, a movable folding screen covered with wallpaper was made of standard hollow-core doors and joined by dual-action hinges. The woodwork of the doorway to the dining room is grained to resemble quarter-sawn oak. At the right in the breakfast room, oxblood-red wainscot panels of Lincrusta with gilded accents are hand-finished to look like tooled-leather panels. Made in England since the 1870s, a good range of embossed wallcoverings remains widely available today.

226. Detail of the dining room in the Victorian flat. Typical of many flats and row houses, this room's only window opens onto a light well. The fireplace retains the original tile surround and the simple wooden mantel has been marbleized. This room's Aesthetic Movement theme is boldly reflected in the frieze that is reproduced from the original in the dining room of the Cohen-Bray House in Oakland (see fig. 95). The Aesthetic theme is also reflected in a Japanesque wallpaper with a cherry blossom motif, in the border used above the chair rail, and in the large four-lobed elements in the frieze. A gilded and stained finish is on the wainscot's embossed Anaglypta.

(Overleaf) 227. Dining room of a Queen Anne row house, San Francisco (c. 1895). The coved ceilings and room-wide angled bay are fairly typical of the Queen Anne style, but framed wall panels and a low wainscot remain from a 1920s remodeling. Within this shell, the owners, who installed the papers themselves, wished to adapt the Gothic Revival style to complement their growing collection of Gothic-style furnishings, objects, and artwork. So two striking wallpaper elements were used: the mural-like Lion and Dove frieze (with its quotation from Isaiah), designed in 1900 by Walter Crane, and the tapestry-like damask pattern adapted from one designed by William Morris, which was set into the panels. The rib-vaulting of a Gothic cathedral inspired the ceiling's radial divisions created by narrow paper borders, with the intersections decorated with paper "bosses."

228. Dining room of an Italianate row house, San Francisco (c.1875). Chopped up for many years as part of a small apartment, this room has been restored to its original configuration. When the lowered ceiling was removed, the original plaster rosette was revealed intact; only minor repairs to the decorative motifs were necessary before it could be painted with colors from the wallpapers. The doors and wainscot were grain-painted like walnut with "burl" in the panels. The complex wallpaper is adapted from a William Morris design, and a crisp 1870s design by Dr. Christopher Dresser was adapted for the frieze. The room's cornice and ceiling moldings were recreated in wood. Wallpaper set into the cove of the cornice continues on the ceiling, where the distinction between raised moldings and wallpaper elements is intentionally blurred.

229. Bedroom of the Spencer House, San Francisco (1896). Above padded upholstered walls used to absorb sound, an unusual frieze and ceiling treatment incorporates wallpaper motifs with an underwater theme. Period originals of the 1880s, discovered in a bedroom closet of a South Dakota farmhouse, include the frieze and the ceiling paper; the border that trims the frieze was adapted to match. Placed in the cove so that light will activate its metallic gold and copper inks, the frieze has a seashell motif in deep rosy mauves that are in striking contrast to the vivid malachite green of the stylized coral forms that entwine around them. The ceiling paper is scattered with stylized pale blue starfish, each delicately outlined in gold. Instead of replacing a missing plaster rosette, a paper medallion was fashioned from single repeats of the frieze and découpaged around the base of the antique ceiling fixture.

230. Breakfast room of the Spencer House. To complement the refined detailing of the elegant oak woodwork, delicate Classical patterns were chosen as the theme for this room's ornament. Executed in a combination of handpainting and stenciling techniques, the freely adapted forms include the palmette motifs set within ovals in the frieze and the stylized flowers that link them together. This room has a wainscot that retains its original that like the woodwork has never been painted. The handsome Lincrusta wainscot has a Classical motif of stylized laurel leaves bound by crossing ribbons. The exceptional hardwood floors are intricately inlaid. The elegant sideboard rejoices in a wealth of delicate carved ornament.

231. Double parlor of the Merguire House, San Francisco (1889). In a Western Addition row house that was originally built by the Rountree Brothers for John L. Merguire, president of the Truckee Lumber Company, this atmospheric space evokes the popular taste of the time. Although the interiors of this house were particularly well-preserved, its owners acquired it with the idea of turning it into a showcase of their period-style interior-design business. Consistent with late Victorian fashion, the room is made invitingly cozy by the stylishly bold color and pattern combinations that have been liberally applied to the floors, walls, and ceilings. The Rococo Revival wallpaper patterns of the walls and frieze are copied from period designs of the 1890s. The draperies are fringed, tasseled, swagged, and festooned in period manner. With lavish applications of color and metallic paint, ornately sculpted plaster ceiling cornices and rosettes, as well as large archway brackets at the room's center and front bay window, contribute to the architectural detail. The fireplace mantel features elaborately turrned spindles rising to the full height of its mirrored overmantel shelves.

232. Dining room of the Merguire House. Emphasizing the importance of the dining room in Victorian households, this room has even more vividly colored wall and frieze patterns than the double parlor. The fireplace retains its original glazed tile surround and an Eastlake mirror is a strong architectural presence over the mantel. Introduced by the wallpaper frieze, a Classical theme continues in a swagged floral pattern set in panels that form the ceiling's central octagon. A massive gold-finished plaster rosette is anchored by the intricate trellis-like pattern in the center panel. Partly visible around the room is the bright gilded finish applied to the original Lincrusta wainscot. To the right of the fireplace is an original servant's call button.

233. Kitchen of the Merguire House. The present charm of this kitchen is a result of the owners' imaginative makeover. Opting for utility, they designed the built-in sideboard at the left, which also created space for a small closet behind the portière at the left and a dumbwaiter on the opposite side. The door next to the stove leads to the dining room, and at the left of the door is a lift-up pass-through. The period telephone at the right of the sideboard works. Adjoining the kitchen through doors on the wall opposite the stove are a small breakfast room and walk-in pantry. The stove is a fully reconditioned Spark model from around 1930 that has a trash burner at the left side.

234. Library of the Merguire House. On the second floor directly above the front half of the double parlor, this room extends the full width of the house to include the bay window at the left and another single window seen in the mantel's Eastlake-style mirror. The owners describe this decorative scheme as a work in progress, but its major elements are substantially complete. Classical themes were considered suitable for Victorian libraries, so the ceiling incorporates panels that reproduce stone friezes of antiquity. Other patterns and borders (some trimmed from the wall patterns) are assembled into a Japanesque collage that reflects Aesthetic taste. Period furnishings include Eastlake chairs, an angled cabinet at the left, and a Renaissance Revival library table.

235. *(Right)* Bedroom of the Merguire House. A substantial Eastlake bedroom set is featured in this room, which is lighted by a combination gas and electric fixture from about 1900 (note the gaslit "candles"). The diagonal form of the plaster ceiling rosette inspired the wallpapered ceiling arrangement. Curvilinear and floral motifs of the frieze, wall fill, and background ceiling patterns reflect the later Rococo Revival style of the 1890s.

236. *(Below)* Bedroom of a Queen Anne-style house, San Francisco (1890). Inspired by the Aesthetic Movement, this room's decorative scheme is defined by motifs taken from nature, for the wallpaper frieze and ceiling designs feature iris and insects. The coved plaster cornice molding has an exotic faux finish that resembles tortoiseshell. Set into the arching cove, a repeating border of moths on a gold ground is set on a delicately gilded checkerboard pattern. Both patterns repeat on the ceiling; outlined by the moth border, angular panels contain two different colorings of a dragonfly and spiderweb pattern. In another Aesthetic touch, the panels are accented by medallions with a sunflower motif. Recessed panels outlined in ebonized moldings distinguish an unusual Eastlake bed with an intricately inlaid footboard. The art-glass door decorated with iris leads to a bathroom. Now operated as a bed-and-breakfast inn called Château Tivoli, this Western Addition house also has an exceptional exterior.

237. Bathroom of the Brune-Reutlinger House, San Francisco (1886). Retaining its original configuration, this bathroom shows that one of the enduring charms of carefully selected fixtures is that they can still function well despite their age. A marble-topped sink on nickel-plated legs is flanked by period wall sconces. The wall-mounted wooden tank of a pull-chain toilet is partially visible to the left of the mirror. Copied from English originals of about 1880, the natural motifs of the wallpaper patterns reflect the Aesthetic Movement then at its peak. These patterns are teeming with life: aquatic reeds and flowers rise from a pebbly bottom, past a flurry of fish. Above the water are birds, butterflies, and dragonflies to enliven the scene, and still more floral patterns reach to the ceiling. At the very top a stylized sunflower sends out rays like a rising sun in a blue sky.

238. Turkish parlor of the Brune-Reutlinger House. This magnificent mélange of Victorian pattern and color rejoices in a lushly wallpapered ceiling centered by a plaster rosette from which hangs an exceptional period gasolier. The original Lincrusta wainscot was finished to match the mostly deep red and gold color scheme, which is complemented by the paper patterns designed with various motifs associated with the Aesthetic Movement. The inclusion of a so-called Turkish parlor in a house was testament to status and worldliness. The same sort of exotic decoration was sometimes applied to rooms that were also called a library, den, or office. Although found in the most respectable of homes, a Turkish parlor was considered a purely male domain. It was a favorite haunt of gentleman visitors and particularly suitable for after-dinner conversation, cigars, and brandy. The lady of the house would probably have had her private retreat, such as a music room or sewing room in which to entertain female guests.

when many of the most prominent companies that supply goods and services to the Victorian Revival market were established. By the 1980s, the serious interest in Victorian houses, neighborhoods, antiques, and decoration had matured into a nationwide movement. This was the decade in which Victorian design became almost an obsession. Historic districts of nineteenth-century houses were established. The finest Victorian antiques became increasingly expensive, so new prominence was given to those of average quality that still had definitive style.

More and more owners of Victorian houses became concerned about what would be historically appropriate for their interiors. Increasing coverage of the period by books and magazines was helpful, but the most zealous old-house fans had to dig further for the best information and resources. Fortunately, specialists in the restoration of historic houses were increasing in almost every community, as were design professionals sympathetic to (and experienced in) historic projects.

Of real importance is the fact that there is a growing strong awareness and real social encouragement to respect and honor our architectural past, rather than ignore it and risk its destruction. Education has certainly helped this process. Across the country there are many instances where people who hadn't previously been "moved" by old buildings have been suddenly mobilized to join in neighborhood activism over the potential loss of an old house or other building. This is a very positive impetus for the preservation movement, and an indication that we are determined to become less of the "throw-away" society that we have been for so long.

Not everyone wants to live in old houses or create atmospheres that evoke the spirit of the past, but those who do are a vocal, opinionated bunch who love to share their passion with others. People who are today immersed in Victorian design have many resources at their command. Never before have so many goods and services been available for the asking, or so many individuals interested in helping to recreate them. The examples illustrated in this chapter are the tip of a national iceberg and only showcase one region's accomplishments, but they will look familiar to many people across the country. There is a universality about Victorian architecture and design in America that causes it to be treasured no matter what the region. The rooms that follow will doubtless provide great enjoyment, if not some sound inspiration, for both old and new devotees of Victoriana. Hopefully, they will also garner some new fans and keep the Victorian Revival on track for the future. One thing is certain: the movement is here to stay.

The many talents that went into each of these rooms deserve special recognition, and those who are known are credited in the back of this book according to the photograph. Unfortunately, many others were probably involved in the projects and will remain uncredited, while others are simply no longer alive to enjoy the credit they deserve. But their work survives, and continues to delight and dazzle as it was intended to, which is perhaps the best legacy of all. Enjoy!

(Overleaf) 239. Front parlor of an Italianate-style house, Alameda, California (1876). To admit more light and views between the rooms, the long, narrow upper panels of the original pocket doors to the dining room (see fig. 240) have been replaced with beveled glass. The pair of later windows, which were retained for the light they provide, await matching art-glass panels. The original high plaster cornice emphasizes the panelized ceiling of raised moldings and Classical cast-plaster ornament. At dado height, a series of panels inset with an Anaglypta pattern are finished like subtly colored tooled leather. The rose-colored willow pattern on the walls was adapted from one by William Morris. The handsome new fireplace mantel was inspired by the large antique Renaissance Revival mirror above, which was imperceptibly adjusted in size to fit the mantel. The rose color of the marble fireplace surround and hearth echoes splendidly the wallpaper color. The antique Renaissance Revival parlor furniture was made by Jeliff.

240. Dining room of the Alameda house. This flamboyant room is at the center of the house and forms the heart of its public spaces. The ceiling is voluptuously rococo with cherubs and painted and gilded cast-plaster ornaments. Adapted from a William Morris design, the walls have a handprinted wallpaper in a richly colored damask pattern with gilded highlights. Its various colors were the source of the palette for the ceiling's moldings, background areas, and various plaster ornaments. The pocket doors to the parlor are to the immediate left. The very large sideboard at the right is a Victorian extravaganza of multiple shelves, columns, drawers, and ebonized carved panels.

241. (Opposite) Conservatory of the Alameda house. This beautiful conservatory was recently created on the second floor, for the owners are avid gardeners. In doing so, they were simply following a popular tradition in large Victorian homes. Entirely roofed in glass, the room has so much light that it was necessary to construct the small Classical "garden temple" at the right to shield excessive sunlight from a collection of delicate orchids. Opposite the temple, French doors open to a covered balcony that overlooks the garden, a large fish pond, and an extensive lawn. The floor is paved with slate. Decorative painting includes the marbleized columns of the temple, the architectural painting at the left above and around the fountain, and on the wall at the right. A glance at the wicker settee shows that this delightful room is the perfect place for a warm catnap.

Listing of Historic House Museums

NOTE: The following house museums apppear in this book, and their style is included for quick reference to the chapter in which each is illustrated. Visitors are most welcome, for the operating budgets of most house museums is dependent on public support. Because the scheduled open hours and admission prices for these houses can vary considerably (and are subject to change), this information is not included here. At most sites, the scheduled days and hours of public access, and the presence of staff to receive visitors and conduct tours, is usually determined by the availability of volunteer docents. All visitors are strongly urged to call in advance to confirm the current schedule of open hours and admission fees, before attempting a visit. Please note that as settings for special occasions some (but not all) of these locations are available on a rental basis. Most of the houses also accept group tour reservations by appointment (planning in advance is required), and sometimes such tours can be arranged for times outside of the regular posted hours.

BOYD GATE HOUSE MUSEUM
Marin County Historical Society
1125 B Street, San Rafael, CA 94901
(415) 454-8538
Style: Gothic Revival

CAMRON-STANFORD HOUSE
Camron-Stanford House Preservation Association
1418 Lakeside Drive, Oakland, CA 94612
(510) 444-1876
Style: Italianate

COHEN-BRAY HOUSE
Victorian Preservation Center of Oakland
1440 29th Avenue, Oakland, CA 94601
(510) 532-0704
Style: Stick / Eastlake Villa

DUNSMUIR HOUSE AND GARDENS
2960 Peralta Oaks Court, Oakland, CA 94605
(510) 615-5555
Style: Colonial / Classical Revival

FALKIRK (Robert Dollar Estate)
Falkirk Cultural Center
1408 Mission Avenue, San Rafael, CA 94901
(415) 485-3328
Style: Queen Anne

FALLON HOUSE (and Peralta Adobe) HISTORIC SITE
175 West St. John Street, San Jose, CA 95110
(408) 993-8182
Style: Italianate (house) and Spanish / Mexican Colonial (adobe)

HAAS-LILIENTHAL HOUSE
San Francisco Architectural Heritage
2007 Franklin Street, San Francisco, CA 94109
(415) 441-3000
Style: Queen Anne

LATHROP HOUSE
Redwood City Heritage Association
627 Hamilton Street, Redwood City, CA 94063
(650) 365-5564
Style: Gothic Revival

LYFORD HOUSE
Richardson Bay Audubon Center & Sanctuary
376 Greenwood Beach Road, Tiburon, CA 94920
(415) 388-2524
Style: Second Empire

McCONAGHY HOUSE
18701 Hesperian Boulevard, Hayward, CA 94541
(510) 276-3010
Style: Stick / Queen Anne Hybrid

JOHN MUIR NATIONAL HISTORIC SITE
4202 Alhambra Avenue, Martinez, CA 94553
(925) 228-8860
Style: Italianate

OCTAGON HOUSE
The National Society of The Colonial Dames of America in
California
2645 Gough Street, San Francisco, CA 94123
(415) 441-7512
Style: Octagon / Italianate Hybrid

PARDEE HOME MUSEUM
672 11th Street, Oakland, CA 94607
(510) 444-2187 (website: www.pardeehome.org)
Style: Italianate Villa

GEORGE W. PATTERSON HOUSE
Ardenwood Regional Park
34600 Ardenwood Boulevard, Fremont, CA 94555
(510) 791-4196
Style: Queen Anne

JAMES SHINN HOUSE
1251 Peralta Avenue, Fremont, CA 94538
(510) 795-0891
Style: Stick / farmhouse vernacular

WINCHESTER HOUSE
The Winchester Mystery House
525 South Winchester Boulevard, San Jose, CA 95128
(408) 247-2000
Style: Queen Anne / Eastlake / Hybrid

OTHER HISTORIC HOUSE MUSEUMS
in the SAN FRANCISCO BAY AREA

NOTE: While it was not possible to photograph every Bay Area house museum for inclusion in this book, there is a significant number of others that are also well worth seeking out. The following list includes most of these additional sites, and each will reward the visitor with its own unique perspective on San Francisco Bay Area history. As previously mentioned for the photographed houses: before attempting a visit, a call in advance to confirm the current schedule of open hours and admission fees for each location is strongly recommended. Many of these sites also offer group tours (by appointment in advance), and some (but not all) are available on a rental basis as settings for special events. In addition to the architectural style of each building, each of these listings also includes the building's construction date after its name.

AINSLEY HOUSE (and Campbell Historical Museum) (1925)
300 Grant Street, Campbell, CA 95008
(408) 866-2118
Style: English Cottage / Tudor Revival

ALVARADO ADOBE (1848; now reconstructed), and
BLUME HOUSE (1905)
1 Alvarado Square / 13831 San Pablo Avenue, San Pablo, CA 94806
(510) 215-3046, or (510) 234-7518
Style: Spanish / Mexican Colonial (adobe); Queen Anne (house)

CASA PERALTA (1897)
San Leandro Historical Society
384 W. Estudillo Avenue, San Leandro, CA 94577
(510) 577-3490
Style: Spanish Colonial Revival (as remodeled)

HARRIS-LASS HISTORIC MUSEUM (c.1870s)
Historic Preservation Society of Santa Clara
1889 Market Street, Santa Clara, CA 95050
(408) 249-7905
Style: Italianate / farmhouse vernacular

KOHL MANSION (1914)
2750 Adeline Drive, Burlingame, CA 94010
(650) 992-4668
Style: English Tudor Revival / "manor"

LOS ALTOS HISTORY HOUSE MUSEUM (c.1910)
51 South San Antonio Road, Los Altos, CA 94023
(415) 948-9427
Style: Shingle / farmhouse vernacular

LUTHER BURBANK HOME AND GARDENS (c.1870s and later)
Santa Rosa Avenue at Sonoma Avenue (P.O. Box 1678), Santa Rosa, CA 95402
(707) 524-5445
Style: Italianate / farmhouse vernacular

MEYERS HOUSE AND GARDEN MUSEUM (1897)
2021 Alameda Avenue, Alameda, CA 94501
(510) 521-1247
Style: Colonial Revival

EUGENE O'NEILL NATIONAL HISTORIC SITE (1937)
P.O. Box 280, Danville, CA 94526
(510) 838-0249
Style: Monterey / Spanish Colonial Revival

YGNACIO PERALTA HOME (ALTA MIRA CLUB) (1860)
Alta Mira Club
561 Lafayette Avenue, San Leandro, CA 94577
(510) 562-7144
Style: Italianate

RALSTON HALL (c.1860s)
College of Notre Dame
1500 Ralston Avenue
Belmont, CA 94002
(650) 508-3501
Style: Italianate Villa

RAVENSWOOD HISTORIC SITE (Cottage: 1885 and Main house: 1891)
2647 Arroyo Road, Livermore, CA 94550
(925) 443-0238
Style: Queen Anne / Eastlake Hybrid

RENGSTORFF HOUSE (1867)
3070 North Shoreline Boulevard, Mountain View, CA 94043
(650) 903-6099
Style: Italianate

SANCHEZ ADOBE (1846)
1000 Linda Mar Boulevard, Pacifica, CA 94044
(650) 359-1462
Style: Spanish / Mexican Colonial (adobe)

SAN JOSE HISTORICAL MUSEUM (c.1880 to c.1930)
1600 Senter Road, San Jose, CA 95112
(408) 287-2290
Style: A mix of various late 19th and early 20th century buildings, including residential, commercial, and agricultural building types, evoke a vintage San Jose "neighborhood."

SHADELANDS RANCH HISTORICAL MUSEUM (1902)
2660 Ygnacio Valley Road, Walnut Creek, CA 94598
(510) 935-7871
Style: Colonial Revival

GENERAL MARIANO VALLEJO HOME ("Lachryma Montis") (c.1851)
West Spain Street at West 3rd Street, Sonoma, CA 95476
(707) 938-9559
Style: Gothic Revival

VILLA MONTALVO (and arboretum) (1912)
15400 Montalvo Road, Saratoga, CA 95071
(408) 961-5800
Style: Mediterranean Villa

Bibliography

Andrews, Wayne. *American Gothic: Its Origins, Its Trials, Its Triumphs*. New York, New York: Vintage Books / Random House, Inc., 1975.

Axelrod, Alan (ed.). *The Colonial Revival in America*. New York, New York, and London, England: W. W. Norton & Company, 1985.

Bagwell, Beth. *Oakland: The Story of a City*. Novato, California: Presidio Press, 1982. Reprint, Oakland, California: Oakland Heritage Alliance, 1996.

Baker, Paul R. *Richard Morris Hunt*. Cambridge, Massachusetts, and London, England: The MIT Press, 1986.

Bernhardi, Robert. *The Buildings of Berkeley*. Oakland, California: Forest Hill Press, 1971.

_____. *The Buildings of Oakland*. Oakland, California: Forest Hill Press, 1979.

Betjeman, John. *A Pictorial History of English Architecture*. New York, New York: The Macmillan Company, 1971.

Bicknell, A.J. *Bicknell's Village Builder and Supplement*. New York, New York: A.J. Bicknell & Co., 1878. Reprint (as *Bicknell's Victorian Buildings*), New York, New York: Dover Publications, Inc., 1979.

Bohn, Dave. *East of These Golden Shores*. Oakland, California: The Junior League of Oakland, and The Scrimshaw Press, 1971.

Brammer, Alex (Intro.). *Victorian Classics of San Francisco*. Sausalito, California: Windgate Press, 1987.

Brechin, Gray. *Imperial San Francisco: Urban Power, Earthly Ruin*. Berkeley and Los Angeles, California: University of California Press, 1999.

Bruegman, Robert. *Benicia: Portrait of an Early California Town*. San Francisco, California: 101 Productions, 1980.

Butler, Phyllis Filiberti. *The Valley of Santa Clara*. San Jose, California: The Junior League of San Jose, 1975. Reprint, Novato, California; Presidio Press, 1981.

Cerny, Susan Dinkelspiel. *Berkeley Landmarks*. Berkeley, California: Berkeley Architectural Heritage Association, 1994.

Clark, Kenneth. *The Gothic Revival*. London, England: Constable, 1928. Reprint, London, England: John Murray, 1978.

Clary, Raymond H. *The Making of Golden Gate Park, 1906-1950*. San Francisco, California: Don't Call It Frisco Press, 1987.

Delehanty, Randolph and Sexton, Richard. *In the Victorian Style*. San Francisco, California: Chronicle Books, 1991.

Dillon, Richard H. *San Francisco: Adventurers and Visionaries*. Tulsa, Oklahoma: Continental Heritage Press, Inc., 1983.

Downing, Alexander Jackson. *The Architecture of Country Houses*. New York, New York: D. Appleton & Company, 1850. Reprint, New York, New York: Dover Publications, Inc., 1969.

Eastlake, Charles L. *Hints on Household Taste*. London, England: Longmans, Green and Company, 1878 (fourth revised edition). Reprint, Mineola, New York: Dover Publications, Inc., 1969.

Fallows, Reverend Samuel (intro). *Complete Story of the San Francisco Horror*. San Francisco, California: Hubert D. Russell, 1906.

Floyd, Margaret Henderson. *Henry Hobson Richardson: A Genius for Architecture*. New York, New York: The Monacelli Press, Inc., 1997.

Fowler, Orson S. *A Home For All, or the Gravel Wall and Octagon Mode of Building*. New York, New York: Fowler and Wells, 1853. Reprint (as A *Home for All)*, New York, New York: Dover Publications, 1973.

Gebhard, David; Sandweiss, Eric; and Winter, Robert. *The Guide to Architecture in San Francisco and Northern California.* Layton, Utah: Gibbs M. Smith, Inc. / Peregrine Smith Books, 1985.

Gere, Charlotte, and Whiteway, Michael. *Nineteenth-Century Design.* London: George Weidenfield and Nicholson Ltd; 1993. Reprint, New York, New York: Harry N. Abrams, Inc., 1994.

Gilliam, Harold, and Bry, Michael. *The Natural World of San Francisco.* Garden City, New York: Doubleday & Company, Inc., 1967.

Girouard, Mark. *Sweetness and Light: The Queen Anne Movement, 1860-1900.* Oxford, England: Clarendon Press, 1977. Reprint, New Haven, Connecticut and London, England: Yale University Press, 1984.

_____. *The Victorian Country House.* New Haven, Connecticut, and London, England: Yale University Press, 1979.

Hansen, Gladys. *San Francisco Almanac.* San Francisco, California: Chronicle Books, 1975.

Heig, James (ed.). *Pictorial History of Tiburon.* San Francisco, California: Scottwall Associates, 1984.

Hitchcock, Henry-Russell. *Early Victorian Architecture In Britain.* New Haven, Connecticut and London, England: Yale University Press, 1954. Reprint, New York, New York: Da Capo Press, Inc., 1976.

Holly, Henry Hudson. *Holly's Country Seats.* New York, New York: D. Appleton and Company, 1863. Reprint (for The Library of Victorian Culture), Watkins Glen, New York: The American Life Foundation & Study Institute, 1977.

_____. *Modern Dwellings.* New York, New York: Harper & Brothers, 1878. Reprint, (for The Library of Victorian Culture), Watkins Glen, New York: The American Life Foundation & Study Institute, 1977.

Keegan, Frank L. *San Rafael: Marin's Mission City.* Northridge, California: Windsor Publications, Inc., 1987.

Kirker, Harold. *California's Architectural Frontier.* San Marino, California: Henry E. Huntington Library and Art Gallery, 1960. Reprint (revised), Santa Barbara and Salt Lake City, Utah: Peregrine Smith, Inc., 1973.

_____. *Old Forms On a New Land: California Architecture in Perspective.* Niwot, Colorado: Roberts Reinhart Publishers, 1991.

Kostoff, Spiro. *A History of Architecture: Settings and Rituals.* New York, New York, and Oxford, England: Oxford University Press, 1985.

Kostura, William. *Russian Hill: The Summit 1853-1906.* San Francisco, California: Aerie Publications, 1997.

_____. *Itinerant Houses: A History of San Francisco's Moving Industry.* San Francisco, California: San Francisco Historical Society, 1999. (an article from *The Argonaut,* Journal of the San Francisco Historical Society, Volume 10, No. 1).

Lewis, Oscar. *San Francisco: Mission to Metropolis.* Berkeley, California: Howell-North Books,1966.

Loewenstein, Louis K. *Streets of San Francisco: The Origins of Street and Place Names.* San Francisco, California: Lexicos, 1984.

Loth, Calder, and Sadler, Julius Trousdale, Jr. *The Only Proper Style: Gothic Architecture in America.* Boston, Massachusetts: New York Graphic Society, 1975.

Maass, John. *The Gingerbread Age.* New York, New York: Reinhart, 1957. Reprint, New York, New York: Greenwich House, 1983.

_____. *The Victorian Home in America.* New York, New York: Hawthorn Books, Inc., 1972.

McAlester, Virginia, and McAlester, Lee. *A Field Guide to American Houses.* New York, New York: Alfred A. Knopf, 1985.

_____. *A Field Guide to America's Historic Neighborhoods and Museum Houses: The Western States.* New York: Alfred A. Knopf, 1998.

McArdle, Alma deC., and McArdle, Dierdre Bartlett. *Carpenter Gothic.* New York, New York: Whitney Library of Design, 1978.

McCoy, Esther. *Five California Architects.* New York, New York: Reinhold Book Corporation, 1960. Reprint, New York, New York: Praeger Publishers, Inc., 1975.

McGrew, Patrick. *Landmarks of San Francisco.* New York, New York: Harry N. Abrams, Inc., 1991.

Mitchell, Eugene. *American Victoriana.* San Francisco, California: Chronicle Books, 1979.

Moss, Roger W. and Winkler, Gail Caskey. *Victorian Exterior Decoration.* New York, New York: Henry Holt and Company, 1987.

Mumford, Lewis. *The Brown Decades: A Study of the Arts in America.* New York, New York: Harcourt, Brace and Company, 1931. Reprint, New York, New York: Dover Publications, Inc., 1971.

Newsom, Samuel and Newsom, Joseph C. *Picturesque California Homes.* San Francisco, California: Samuel and Joseph C. Newsom, Architects and Publishers, 1884. Reprint, Los Angeles, California: Hennessey & Ingalls, Inc., 1978.

Olwell, Carol, and Waldhorn, Judith Lynch. *A Gift to the Street.* New York, New York: St. Martin's Press, 1976.

Regnery, Dorothy F. *An Enduring Heritage.* Stanford, California: Stanford University Press, 1976.

Richey, Elinor. *The Ultimate Victorians*. Berkeley, California: Howell-North Books, 1970.

Scully, Vincent J. Jr. *The Shingle Style and the Stick Style*. New Haven, Connecticut, and London, England: Yale University Press, 1955; revised edition, 1971.

Shoppell, R.W., et al. *Turn-of-the-Century Houses, Cottages and Villas*. New York, New York: Dover Publications, Inc., 1983.

Shortridge, Charles M. (ed.). *Sunshine, Fruit and Flowers*. San Jose, California: San Jose Mercury Publishing and Printing Co., 1896. Reprint, San Jose, California: The San Jose Historical Museum Association, 1986.

Sloan, Samuel. *The Model Architect* (volumes I & II). Philadelphia, Pennsylvania: E.S. Jones & Co., 1852. Reprint (as *Sloan's Victorian Buildings*), New York, New York: Dover Publications, 1980.

Vail, Wesley D. *Victorians: An Account of Domestic Architecture in Victorian San Francisco, 1870-1890*. San Francisco, California: Wesley D. Vail, 1964.

Van Rensselaer, Mariana. *Henry Hobson Richardson and His Works*. New York, New York: Houghton, Mifflin and Company, 1888. Reprint, New York, New York: Dover Publications, Inc., 1969.

Vaux, Calvert. *Villa and Cottage Architecture*. New York, New York: Harper & Brothers, 1864. Reprint, Mineola, New York: Dover Publications, Inc., 1991.

Waldhorn, Judith Lynch; Woodbridge, Sally B. *Victoria's Legacy*. San Francisco, California: 101 Productions, 1978.

Walker, Lester. *American Shelter*. Woodstock, New York: The Overlook Press, 1981.

Watkins, T.H. *California: An Illustrated History*. New York, New York: American Legacy Press, 1983.

Wilson, Mark A. *A Living Legacy*. San Francisco, California: Lexicos, 1987.

Wilson, Richard Guy. *McKim, Mead & White, Architects*. New York, New York: Rizzoli International Publications, Inc., 1983.

Wollenberg, Charles. *Golden Gate Metropolis*. Berkeley, California: Institute of Governmental Studies, University of California, 1985.

Woodbridge, Sally Byrne., and Woodbridge, John Marshall. *San Francisco Architecture*. San Francisco, California: Chronicle Books, 1992.

Woodbridge, Sally B. *California Architecture*. San Francisco, California: Chronicle Books, 1988.

Young, John P. *San Francisco: A History of the Pacific Coast Metropolis*. (volumes I & II) San Francisco, California, and Chicago, Illinois: The S.J. Clarke Publishing Company, 1912.

Resources

As part of today's Victorian Revival movement, some examples of home furnishings, finishes, and other related products that appear in this book are currently available for the restoration and remodeling of historic homes. A growing selection of specialized product lines created by individual artisans, craftspeople, small workshops, and also larger manufacturers across the country offers a wide range of products geared toward Victorian-era houses. Many of these companies sell their services or wares nationally, often by mail order, while others prefer to do business on a smaller scale or on a more local level.

Rather than attempt to assemble a definitive list of every noteworthy Victorian-related resource available to homeowners and design professionals today, we have instead opted to include a brief listing of periodicals that specialize in (or feature regular coverage of) Victorian-related architecture, design, and interior furnishings. Readers will find that many of the resources that sell their wares nationally are also regular advertisers in many of these periodicals. By consulting them routinely for the latest information, readers will be able to learn about the most current products and their manufacturers, as well as updated business addresses, telephone and fax numbers, e-mail and website addresses. Finding reputable specialized resources that may be available only within individual communities (or in their immediate vicinity) may require a bit of local sleuthing. For such information to be the most reliable, it is always best to obtain a personal recommendation or referral from someone who has already utilized the resource and was pleased with the results. Whenever possible, it is also helpful to be able to ask questions and view examples of previous work in person.

Related Periodicals:

Old House Interiors
108 East Main Street
Gloucester, MA 01930
(800) 356-9313
www.oldhouseinteriors.com

Old House Journal
One Thomas Circle NW
Washington, D.C. 20005
(800) 234-3797
www.oldhousejournal.com

Period Homes
69-A Seventh Avenue
Brooklyn, NY 11217
FAX: (718) 636-0750
www.period-homes.com

Preservation
c/o National Trust for Historic Preservation
1785 Massachusetts Avenue, N.W.
Washington, D.C. 20036
(800) 944-6847
Note: A subscription to *Preservation* is a benefit of membership in the National Trust.

Nineteenth Century
c/o The Victorian Society in America
219 South Sixth Street
Philadelphia, PA 19106
(215) 627-4252
Note: A subscription to *Nineteenth Century* is a benefit of membership in the Victorian Society in America.

This Old House Magazine
1185 Avenue of the Americas
New York, NY 10036
(800) 898-7237
www.thisoldhouse.org

Traditional Building
69-A Seventh Avenue
Brooklyn, NY 11217
FAX: (718) 636-0750
www. traditional-building.com

Victorian Decorating and Lifestyle
419 Park Avenue South, 18th Floor
New York, NY 10016
(212) 541-7100
www.victoriandecorandlife.com

Victorian Homes
265 South Anita Drive, Suite 120
Orange, CA 92868
(714) 939-9991

Credits

This list credits the efforts of various design professionals, artisans, craftspersons, and manufacturers whose work is featured in the following photographs. At the time this book went to press, some names deserving of credit may have remained absent from this list. Our sincere apologies are extended to anyone whose work remains uncredited; we do greatly appreciate the contributions of all who helped save and beautify these historic houses.

Figs. 1, 4, 191, 203, 204, 205, 207: Façade design and restoration: Clearheart / Skeeter Jones. Figs. 48, 131, 134, 180, 181: Color consultant: Jill Pilaroscia. Fig. 48: Exterior design and restoration: Erik Kramvik; Seismic upgrading and foundation work: Winans Construction / Paul and Nina Winans. Fig. 56: Color and front-door design: Erik Kramvik; front-door fabrication: Scott Wynn; Painting contractor: Magic Brush / Robert Dufort. Figs. 57, 81, 101, 104, 105, 106, 107, 116, 133, 160, 166, 182, 183, 187: Color consultant: Bob Buckter. Fig. 106: Painting contractor: Cal Crew. Figs. 48, 75, 103, 131, 182, 183: Painting contractor: Local Color / Bruce Nelson. Fig. 58: Color consultant: Tony Caneletich; Painting contractor: Cal Crew. Fig. 61: Wallpaper: Bradbury & Bradbury. Fig. 62: Wallpaper: Zina. Fig. 65: Stenciling: Larry Boyce. Fig. 134: Painting contractor: Color Quest / Paul Kensinger. Figs. 180, 181: Painting contractor: Magic Brush / Robert Dufort. Fig. 184: Color consultant: Butch Kardum. Figs. 185, 186: Color consultant: Lynne Rutter. Fig. 189: Façade design / restoration: Scott Wynn. Fig. 77: bracket design / fabrication: Erik Kramvik; turned finials: Gail Redman. Fig. 117, 118, 119, 120: Interior-design consultant: Paul Duchscherer; Wallpaper: Bradbury & Bradbury; Wallpaper installation: Helen Boutell. Preservation architect: Arnold Lerner, A.I.A.; General contractor for restoration: Plath & Company. Figs. 193, 194: Interior restoration by Artistic License of San Francisco; Interior design consultant: Paul Duchscherer; Color consultant: Bob Buckter; Surface preparation, finish painting / pinstriping: Local Color / Bruce Nelson and Magic Brush / Robert Dufort. Wallpaper: Bradbury & Bradbury; decorative-plasterwork painted finishes: Ruby Newman; Stenciling and bay-window ceiling painting: George Zaffle; Marbleizing (of columns): Joni Monnich; Wallpaper installation: Peter Bridgman (ceiling) and Helen Boutell (walls); Bay-window valance / design: Erik Kramvik; fabrication: Scott Wynn; installation: Winans Construction / Paul and Nina Winans; plaster ornament: Lorna Kollmeyer. Cabinetwork (new pier-mirror base): William Eichenberger; Picture molding / metal-leaf finish: Frances Binnington. Fig. 198: Façade design: Erik Kramvik; Wood rail and finial turnings: Gail Redman; Columns: Haas Wood & Ivory Works; General Contractor: Winans Construction / Paul and Nina Winans. Fig. 200: Façade and fence design: Rynerson O'Brien Architecture / Steve Rynerson. Fig. 207: Color consultant: James Bernstein; Painting contractor: Local Color / Bruce Nelson. Fig. 209: Façade design and restoration: Rynerson O'Brien / Steve Rynerson. Figs. 211, 213: Color Consultant: Bob Buckter. Fig. 213: Painting contractor: Local Color / Bruce Nelson. Fig. 215: Wood carving: David Keller. Fig. 155: Restoration design: Rynerson O'Brien Architecture; General Contractor: Winans Construction / Paul and Nina Winans. Figs. 218, 219, 220, 221, 222: Interior designer: David Modell; Staircase restoration and inlaid hardwood floors: Hector Villanueva; Stenciling design and execution: Larry Boyce & Associates (including Tom Ciesla, Ken Huse, and George Zaffle); Graining: John Seekamp; Painted wall / wainscot finishes: Michael Shiell; Carpet: Scalamandre. Fig 220: Wallpaper: Bradbury & Bradbury; Wallpaper installation: Holly Fisher; Carpet: Scalamandre. Glass door panels: Andreas Lehmann and Thomas Tisch. Fig. 221: Hardware fabrication: Eric Clausen. Figs. 223, 224, 225, 226, 227, 228, 229, 237, 238: Wallpaper: Bradbury & Bradbury; Interior designer: Paul Duchscherer (while Design Service Director at Bradbury & Bradbury), with design assistance by staff including Cheryl Gordon, Therese Tierney, Diana Woodbridge, and Rob Anderson. Fig. 223: Wallpaper Installation: Peter Bridgman; Painted plasterwork: Ruby Newman. Fig. 224: Wallpaper installation: Peter Bridgman. Marbleizing (fireplace mantel): Joni Monnich. Figs. 225, 237: Wallpaper installation: Helen Boutell. Fig. 225: Painted finishes: Joni Monnich; Wainscot: Lincrusta / Crown Corporation. Fig. 226: Wallpaper installation, graining, and other painted finishes: Return to Splendor / Zane Working and Mark Egeland. Wainscot: Supaglypta / Crown Corporation. Fig. 227: Wallpaper installation: David and Virginia Keller. Figs. 228, 229, 237, 238, 239: Wallpaper installation: Peter Bridgman. Fig. 228: Plaster rosette restoration: Lorna Kollmeyer; Graining: Joni Monnich. Figs. 229, 230: Antique lighting by Illustrious Lighting / John Isola. Fig. 230: Stenciling design and execution: Larry Boyce & Associates (including Tom Ciesla, Ken Huse, and George Zaffle). Figs. 231, 232, 233, 234, 235: Interior design, wallpaper installation, decorative painting and furnishings by Victorian Interiors / Larkin Mayo and Gary Yuschalk. Wallpaper (combined patterns from various manufacturers): Victorian Collectibles, J.R. Burrows & Company, Carter & Company, Bradbury & Bradbury, and Scalamandre. Figs. 239, 240, 241: Interior design: Paul Duchscherer and Erik Kramvik. Figs. 239, 240: Wallpaper: Bradbury & Bradbury; Wallpaper installation: Peter Bridgman. Cast ceiling ornaments: Decorator's Supply Corporation. Ceiling moldings: OracDecor; Ceiling molding installation: Peter Post. Graining: Norman Rizzi; Other painted finishes (including trompe l'oeil ceiling painting): Ruby Newman. Wall panel insets: Supaglypta / Crown Corporation; Fig. 239: Antique mirror and parlor seating: J. Hill Antiques. Fireplace / mantel fabrication: William Eichenberger. Fireplace surround: San Francisco Marble Company. Fig. 241: Painted finishes (including trompe l'oeil wall painting): George Zaffle. Carpentry: Patrick Kirkhuff; Cast keystone face: Design Toscano; Woodturning (columns): Gail Redman. Title page(s): Interior design/coordination: Paul Duchscherer; Wallpaper: Bradbury & Bradbury; Wallpaper installation: Peter Bridgman; Plaster painted finishes: Ruby Newman.